Getting Ready to Read

D1562304

Book 1

OTHER GOODYEAR BOOKS IN LANGUAGE ARTS & READING

DO YOU READ ME? *Practical Approaches to Teaching Reading Comprehension*
Arnold A. Griese

I CAN MAKE IT ON MY OWN *Functional Reading Ideas and Activities for Daily Survival*
Michelle Berman and Linda Shevitz

GALAXY OF GAMES *For Reinforcing Writing Skills*
Jerry Mallett

IMAGINE THAT! *Illustrated Poems and Creative Learning Experiences*
Joyce King and Carol Katzman

LANGUAGE ARTS IDEA BOOK *Classroom Activities for Children*
Joanne Schaff

MAINSTREAMING LANGUAGE ARTS AND SOCIAL STUDIES *Special Ideas and Activities for the Whole Class*
Anne H. Adams, Charles R. Coble, Paul B. Hounshell

MAKING KIDS CLICK *Independent Activities in Reading and the Language Arts*
Linda Polon and Aileen Cantwell

NEW DIMENSIONS IN ENGLISH *An Ideabook of Language Arts Activities for Middle and Secondary School Teachers*
Joanne Schaff

AN OUNCE OF PREVENTION PLUS A POUND OF CURE *Tests and Techniques for Aiding Individual Readers*
Ronald W. Bruton

PHORGAN'S PHONICS
Harry W. Forgan

READING CORNER *Ideas, Games, and Activities for Individualizing Reading*
Harry W. Forgan

READ ALL ABOUT IT *Using Interests and Hobbies to Motivate Young Readers*
Harry W. Forgan

SUCCESS IN READING AND WRITING SERIES
Anne H. Adams, Elizabeth Bebensee, Helen Cappleman, Judith Connors, Mary Johnson

READING FOR SURVIVAL IN TODAY'S SOCIETY *Volumes I and II*
Anne H. Adams, Anne Flowers, Elsa E. Woods

TOTALACTION *Ideas and Activities for Teaching Children Ages Five to Eight*
Pat Short and Billee Davidson

WRITE UP A STORM *Creative Writing Ideas and Activities for the Middle Grades*
Linda Polon and Aileen Cantwell

WRITING CORNER
Arnold Cheyney

For information about these or other Goodyear books in Science, Math, Social Studies, General Methods, and Centers, write to

Janet Jackson
Goodyear Publishing Company
1640 Fifth Street
Santa Monica, CA 90401
(213) 393-6731

Getting Ready to Read

Book 1

Harry W. Forgan, Ph.D.

M. Liz Christman-Rothlein, Ed.D.

Both of the University of Miami
Coral Gables, Florida

Goodyear Publishing Company, Inc.
Santa Monica, California

Library of Congress Cataloging in Publication Data

FORGAN, HARRY W.
    Getting ready to read.

    (Goodyear series in education)
    Authors' names in reverse order in book 2.
    1. Reading readiness. I. Christman—Rothlein, M.
Liz, joint author. II. Title.
LB1050.43.F67   372.4'142   80–23366
ISBN 0–8302–3390–3 (book 1)
ISBN 0–8302–3390–1 (book 2)

This book is dedicated to those people who make living a joy—

Liz's daughters, Kim and Terri, and her husband, Ash

and in memory of John Strickler, friend and Professor of
Education at the University of Miami.

Y–3390–5

Current printing (last digit)
10 9 8 7 6 5 4 3 2 1

Cover Design: Karen McBride
Composition: Graphic Typesetting Service

Printed in the United States of America

Contents

Preface

This book is intended for use by teachers, parents, day care center workers, or anyone involved in reading readiness programs for three- to six-year-old children. It is designed to help in determining and developing the perceptual skills of students in light of their readiness for reading. Specifically, the book provides diagnostic devices to help determine the visual-motor coordination, auditory skills, and visual skills that young children must develop before they begin to read and instructional ideas and materials that will aid in furthering the development of these skills.

Each one of the three perceptual areas is divided into three levels of performance. For example, for the auditory skills, at the first level of performance the child is able to hear differences in environmental sounds. At the second level of performance the child can discriminate sounds in the initial position of words and remember three unrelated words in sequence. At the third level of performance the child is able to discriminate rhyming words and can remember four unrelated words in sequence. As you read the descriptions of the levels of performance for each one of the three prereading areas, you will begin to understand how children gradually develop readiness for reading.

After you understand the different levels of performance for the perceptual skills that are required for initial reading instruction, you can determine the prereading needs of your students. Chapter 2 presents several techniques for assessing the perceptual skill needs of children including a ready-to-use Home Information Report and several skills tests. You have permission to duplicate all of these materials for use with your students and their parents. In addition to the informal methods of diagnosis, chapter 2 also includes a list of appropriate standardized tests.

The third chapter in the book includes ready-to-make activities for helping children develop the perceptual skills. Activities are provided for each level of performance for each one of the three perceptual skill areas: visual-motor coordination, auditory skills, and visual skills. Making the activities does require some time, but you can often get help from parents and older students and your efforts will be worthwhile, as you will find the students truly enjoying the activities again and again. As one five-year-old child told us, "The games are fun—they are not school!"

Since teachers cannot make all of the activities that are needed to help children develop the perceptual skills, chapter 4 consists of lists of eighty additional activities and forty-eight commercial materials that can be used to help young children develop the prerequisite skills. The additional materials and ideas are ones that can be used by both teachers and parents. The list of eighty ideas will be especially helpful in selecting appropriate instructional activities to use with particular children.

It is important to remember that this book deals with only three of the six major prereading skills. The other major prereading skills—concept development, oral language development and readiness for books—are covered in our companion book, *Getting Ready to Read: Book 2*. This second volume is also published by Goodyear Publishing Company and follows the same format as this book in terms of presenting ready-to-use diagnostic devices and instructional materials and ideas.

There are several people who helped us in writing this book and we would like to acknowledge their time and efforts. A very special word of thanks is extended to Minette Douglas and Pam Russo, who field tested the materials with children at the Canterbury Day Care Center on the University of Miami campus. The children at the center who participated in the field testing were delightful and kept us on task with their positive comments and beautiful smiles. There is one five-year-old girl to whom we would like to extend a special word of appreciation—Jenny Forgan. She field tested every idea in this book!

Many people helped us in preparing the manuscript. Most importantly, we would like to acknowledge Laurie Greenstein, who so carefully guided the manuscript through the various stages of production. Gratitude is extended to Lyn Russo and Suzy Breitner for making many line drawings for the illustrations. Marge Kelley typed many of the rough copies of the manuscript and aided in duplication. As usual, Ruth Ann Forgan typed and retyped the final manuscript without complaining about revisions. Our spouses, Ruth Ann and Ash, deserve special thanks as they did not laugh or complain when we had Magic Markers, folders, glue, and many activities all around the house!

ONE
ONE
ONE
ONE
ONE

INTRODUCTION

HELPING CHILDREN DEVELOP READINESS FOR READING

While visiting a school last week we noticed a group of young children browsing through books in the library. We spotted Joni, a charming, wide-eyed, curly-headed little girl we had worked with at Canterbury Day Care Center. She appeared to be very serious and intent about choosing a book.

When Joni noticed we were watching her, she smiled at us so we walked over and greeted her. Joni began to share her book with us, pointing to pictures and telling us about them saying such things as, "This is a bus. I ride my bus to school." In doing this, Joni was demonstrating knowledge of both concept development and oral language, two important prerequisites to reading. Concept development helped Joni bring meaning to the printed page; she was able to identify the bus and know what it was used for. Also, Joni was able to orally express herself by using sentences to tell us about the pictures.

As we watched her, we noticed she knew the back of the book from the front, the top from the bottom, and seemed to have no difficulty turning the pages. It was obvious she had acquired another of the pre-reading skills—readiness for books.

As we browsed through the book with Joni she seemed so proud as she pointed to letters saying, "This is a b, this is an m," and so forth. She even read some words such as man, cat, and hat. In doing this Joni was using some of the visual skills necessary for beginning reading. We asked Joni if she knew any other words that sounded like cat and bat. She responded, "Sure, bat, sat, and fat! Oh yeah, and rat." She seemed very pleased with herself as she displayed the auditory skills that are so significant as a prerequisite to reading.

As we were about to leave, Joni suggested that she would read the story to us. She proceeded to "read" the book by telling us a story using the pictures, occasionally pointing to a word and saying it. As she "read" the story to us her eyes moved from left-to-right indicating good visual-motor coordination.

1

What a rewarding experience! Here was a child who was enjoying the process of learning to read. Before Joni could "read" her book there were many perceptual skills she had to develop in order to perceive the words and the messages the words convey. Joni had to be able to see and hear differences and similarities in words and she had to be able to follow a printed line of symbols without losing her place.

THE SIX MAJOR PREREADING SKILLS

There are many prereading skills that are gradually developed in order to make it possible for children to read books. This book covers three of the major prereading skills: visual motor coordination, auditory skills, and visual skills. Our companion book, *Getting Ready to Read: Book 2*, deals with concept development, oral language development, and readiness for books. There are other prerequisites for reading, such as the ability to work cooperatively with the teacher and peers; however our books are concerned with the cognitive, affective, and psychomotor skills that are prerequisites for reading rather than the socioemotional attributes of the children. Let us briefly examine each of these six areas so you will have a better idea of the purpose of these books.

Being able to follow a printed line of symbols is necessary for reading. The children must have adequate *visual-motor coordination* in order to do this. Since reading and writing words are so closely related and frequently taught at the same time, the children also must have the necessary visual-motor skills to write the letters and words that they are learning. The child whose eyes do not work together is going to have difficulty when attempting to read.

The *auditory skills* that the children have developed also make a difference in determining whether or not they are ready for reading instruction. The children must be able to hear differences in the sounds of the English language. This is more difficult than it seems because many of the sounds, such as /t/ and /d/, are similar. Of course, the children must not only be able to hear the differences represented by separate letters, but also differences in words that sound alike at the beginning but are different at the end, such as bad and bat. The children must also be able to remember the sounds so they can reproduce them and blend them together to make words.

Reading is basically a visual process that requires children to look carefully at letters and words and then relate them to their oral language. Before children can read there are many *visual skills* they must develop. In the English language, there are only twenty-six letters. However, many of the letters have a different form for upper case and lower case, many of the letters are very similar (such as b, d, p, and q), and other letters are simply reversed (such as u and n). These distinctions add to the difficulty of learning to recognize the letters. Also, just recognizing differences in isolated letters is not enough for beginning reading. The children must be able to see differences in words, too. Well-developed visual skills are necessary to see differences between words such as Sam and see.

Concept development is one of the most important prereading skills. Before children can perceive meaning from a printed page, they must bring meaning to it. During the first few years of life, children develop many concepts by exploring and using the five senses. It is fascinating to watch children pick up some object, hit it against another, smell it, bite it, feel it, shake it, and look at the different sides of the object. Children who have many opportunities to explore objects begin to see likenesses, differences, and relationships among the various objects. Soon the children become aware of many different colors, sizes, number concepts, names of letters, types of clothing, and other classifications.

Another major prereading skill that is gradually developed, beginning at birth, is *oral language*. Babies announce their arrival with a cry, and then begin to listen carefully to the sounds around them. Infants soon can make other sounds that lead up to coherent speech. Before children can learn to read, they must be able to talk. The children must realize that words can be put together to form sentences that relay messages. Of course, the sentences become more and more complex as the children listen to other people speak. Likewise, the children are able to say many more words as they gradually develop the ability to reproduce the forty-five sounds of the English language.

Parents and teachers can introduce children to books, but they can't make the children read. Children must have the desire to read, or the teacher's attempts in working with the children will be in vain. Thus, the sixth major prereading skill is *readiness for books*. The children who enjoy listening to others tell stories and pretend to be reading are likely to succeed when they try to "really read" that first book!

In summary, it is a combination of prerequisite skills, knowledge, and attitudes that enables children to read. To help children become ready to read it is necessary to develop all of the specific skills required. The purpose of this book is to help you identify and provide for the prereading needs of your students for three of the six prereading skills.

LEVELS OF PERFORMANCE

In order to help children develop adequate perceptual skills, it is necessary to identify the tasks related to those skills that the children can perform. For example, when the visual skills are considered, one must see what types of visual stimuli children are able to perceive. At the lowest level of performance for visual skills, a child should be able to see differences in geometric shapes such as a circle and a square. At the second level of performance, the child should be able to see differences in isolated letters such as m and n. At the third level of performance, the child should be able to see differences in words such as on and an. Of course, our concern is helping children develop the visual skills at the third level so as to enable them to read.

It is possible to subdivide the levels of performance for each of the perceptual areas into many categories; however, we believe three very distinctly different levels of performance will be sufficient to enable you to pinpoint the specific prereading needs of young children. Level one is generally characteristic of three-year-old children, level two of four-year-olds, and level three of five- and six-year-old children.

The development of each one of these perceptual prereading skills begins at birth, and continues for many years beyond the prereading stage, but for the purposes of this book we will only deal with the development of prereading skills by children in the three- to six-year-old age group. Let us now examine the three levels of performance for each one of the three perceptual skill areas: visual-motor coordination, auditory skills, and visual skills.

VISUAL-MOTOR COORDINATION

The development of the visual-motor coordination skills is gradual. At the first level of performance, children are able to control their large muscles as required for running and hopping. Fine motor coordination is slower to develop and children at this level have a difficult time staying within the lines when they color and difficulty buttoning their clothes. At this stage children are very active and enjoy imitating the walks of different animals such as elephants, gorillas, and ducks. Children also enjoy experimenting with their body movements by hopping on one foot and then the other, walking backwards, and trying to gallop even though they may not be well coordinated.

As children mature physically, their visual-motor coordination improves. Children at the second level of performance can generally connect dots when the dots are one inch apart. They are able to reproduce a circle easily and can make the lines of a triangle and square meet. (The square may not be exactly square when they reproduce it, but an adult observer can identify it.) At this second level of performance, children are able to turn pages of a book carefully and usually want to write their own names.

At the third level of performance, children are generally able to copy most of the letters of the alphabet. They still may have some difficulty in making letters with several lines, such as k and N, but generally they are able to reproduce the letters and most numerals so adults can identify them. In reproducing letters and numerals they may write some backwards. For example, many children reverse the shapes of s, 5, or b. Teachers should keep in mind that many letters of our alphabet are very similar and it is common for children to reverse them when first learning to write them. This reversing will usually stop when the children get older. At this stage of visual-motor coordination, children are also able to use a pair of scissors to cut on a straight line. They may move a quarter or a half inch off the lines at times, but they are able to cut a picture out of a newspaper or magazine.

Visual-motor coordination continues to improve even after children begin to learn to read words. The major concern at the third level of performance is that the children are able to follow a printed line of symbols. If the initial reading program requires the children to write words and sentences as they are learning to read them, the development of the ability to copy letters and write words also will be important.

AUDITORY SKILLS

The three levels of performance for auditory skills can be distinguished by the kinds of auditory stimuli children are able to discriminate and remember. At the first level of performance of auditory skills, children are able to distinguish gross environmental sounds such as a bell ringing, paper crumbling, or the sounds of various animals. Children are becoming aware of the many different sounds in their environment and are fascinated by the sounds objects make when they are hit against one another. Children are also able to remember simple rhythmic patterns such as when the teacher goes clap-clap-clap, or clap-pause-clap.

At the second level of performance for auditory skills, children are able to hear similarities and differences in sounds of letters that occur in the initial position of words. For example, a child is able to tell you that sun and soap sound alike at the beginning, whereas hat and bat have a different sound at the beginning. The importance of auditory skills, as far as beginning reading instruction is concerned, is apparent when phonics is emphasized. Before children can learn to associate a particular sound with a symbol, they must be able to clearly discriminate that sound from others.

Of course, some sounds are more difficult to discriminate than others; thus, there may be some sounds children are not yet able to discriminate. For example, many children have difficulty in discriminating the voiced th as in the word that and the voiceless th as in the word thing. Children who have difficulty discriminating certain sounds may rely on the context. A child who has difficulty discriminating the two sounds of th will be able to tell from the context what the missing words are in the sentence, "I want --at --ing." The child will realize the sentence is "I want that thing," based on the context and the other sounds in the words. As we help children discriminate different sounds, we must realize some of the sounds are easily confused, but there are other clues that the children can use if they are having difficulty.

At the second level of performance, children also should be able to remember a sequence of three unrelated words. For example, if you said to a child, "Listen carefully as I say these words, and repeat them back to me in the same order," and continued by saying, "cat, pencil, sky," the child should be able to repeat the words in sequence. Auditory memory is important so children can reproduce and blend two, three, and four syllable words that they are learning, such as breakfast, tomorrow, and automobile.

At the third level of performance for auditory skills, children are able to discriminate words that rhyme and are able to hear similarities and differences in the medial and final position of words. If you ask a child if sit and sat rhyme, the child should be able to tell you they do not. Conversely, if you ask the child if pan and man rhyme, the child should be able to tell you they do. Being able to hear rhyming words is very important in beginning reading instruction because many of the words in the beginning books have similar sound patterns, such as bat, cat, hat, fat, pat, rat, sat, and that.

At the third stage of performance for auditory skills, we are also concerned about auditory memory. Children who have reached the third stage are generally able to remember a sequence of four unrelated numerals or words. If you say to a child, "Repeat after me," and then say, "one, seven, ten, and three," the child is able to say them back to you in the same order. Auditory memory is important because children are learning many multisyllabic words and they must be able to remember the different syllables and blend them together. Of course, children must be able to remember sequences of directions, too.

We would like to offer a word of caution concerning the development of the prereading skills. Keep in mind that some children have difficulty producing sounds such as /wh/, /j/, /th/, /th/, /v/, /l/, and /b/ until the age of six or seven. These children may learn several sight words and still not be able to discriminate all of the sounds of the English language. Remember that the prereading skills continue to be refined and extended even after the children begin to read many words.

VISUAL SKILLS

Since reading is a visual process, children must be able to see differences in letter forms and remember letter forms. Thus, there are two basic objectives associated with helping children develop the visual skills necessary for reading: (1) to be able to discriminate differences among the letters and words, and (2) to be able to remember the shapes or forms of letters and words. As simple as this may seem to us as adults, many young children have difficulty seeing differences among letters and in remembering the shapes of letters. This is particularly true with the English alphabet in that many of the letters are similar in configuration because they are formed with variations of circles and straight lines. For example, the letter o can become an a, b, d, g, or p simply by adding lines to it.

At first it may seem that our responsibility is simply to teach children to discriminate among the twenty-six letters in our alphabet, but when the capital letters as well as the lower-case letters are considered, the number of discriminations increases. Many of the lower-case letters are different from their corresponding upper-case letters, as in the case with A and a, D and d, G and g, Q and q, or R and r. We are also teaching children to discriminate and remember many letter forms that differ in various forms of printing, such as a and a.

At the first level of performance for visual skills, children are able to see and remember geometric shapes that are grossly different. At this level if you show a child three circles and a square, the child will be able to point to the one that is different. This type of activity helps the child learn the meaning of same and different.

At the second level of performance, children are able to discriminate and remember letter forms in isolation. If you show a child three t's and an l, the child at this level will be able to tell you which one is different. This is a higher level of performance than simply discriminating geometric shapes. Also at this level of performance children are usually able to recognize their own names.

At the highest level of performance, the third level, children are able to discriminate words. For example, if you show a child the words that, that, than, and that, the child will be able to tell you which one is different. At the third level of performance children should be able to discriminate words that are different either at the beginning, medial, and/ or final positions, such as in bat and pat, bet and bat, and bed and beg. In addition to visually discriminating words, the children will be able to remember a minimum of three letters in sequence. Since many of the words beginning readers learn are three-letter words, it is essential for them to be able to remember a sequence of three letters before they can actually begin to read.

Helping children progress from one level of performance to a higher level of performance in terms of the visual skills is of major importance. If not enough attention is paid to the visual skills, the children will have a difficult time in beginning reading. They will especially confuse words that are somewhat similar such as bad and dad, what and when, how and now, went and want, and store and stove. To prevent children from looking at the configuration of the word and guessing what it might be, make sure enough time is spent helping the children to look carefully at each letter in the word and to notice differences.

As mentioned earlier, the prereading skills are developed gradually from birth and continue to be developed beyond the age of six. For example, it is common for some children to confuse words such as was and saw, on and no, and other words that are easily reversed until the age of eight. Usually the children who do this are able to use context clues to determine what the word is. For example, a child will use context to discriminate was or saw, as in the following sentences:

1. The boy _____the truck. (saw)
2. The boy _____climbing the tree. (was)

It is possible, then, for children to learn to read many words before they are able to discriminate all words.

In summary, let us reiterate our earlier statement that children will continue to improve in all of these prereading areas even after they begin to read some words. Children may not be at level three in all the pre-reading skills when they begin reading some words. Some children may be at level two in an area, and still be ready for reading instruction. For example, a child may be at level two in auditory skills, but have an excellent visual memory and thus be able to learn many words by sight. Another child may have extreme difficulty in writing certain letters, yet is able to read words containing those letters.

The most important guideline that we would like you to remember is that of ensuring success for the beginning reader. Recently there has been so much emphasis on early reading instruction that some of the necessary prerequisites for reading have been overlooked. The result has been that some children are frustrated with their initial experiences in learning to read. These children are the ones who are asked to read words before they are able to see or hear differences in the words, and/or follow a printed line of symbols. The poem, "I Don't Like School Anymore," illustrates the feelings of a five- or six-year-old child who was being asked to read without having developed the necessary prerequisites.

I Don't Like School Anymore

I don't like school anymore!
I used to like it, but now it's a bore.
We used to play with blocks and things,
And everyday we would take time to sing.
But not anymore—
School is a bore.
We have to read these dumb little books;
I can't keep my place as hard as I look.
We used to make things from clay;
I couldn't wait until the next day.
Now the teacher shows us words;
We never get clay to make animals and birds.
School used to be fun, but not anymore.
The teacher says we've got to learn to read,
And that's something I just don't need.
I told the teacher, and she says reading will help us get ahead,
But I don't care—my mom reads to me before I go to bed.
I don't want to get ahead;
I just want to listen to a story instead.
I don't like school anymore,
It really is a bore!
Why doesn't the teacher make school fun?
Why can't we ever go out to play in the sun?
I used to like school when there were puzzles and games;
Now the teacher says she has "specific aims."
I'm tired of all this,
I can't wait until I'm eight,
Then I'll quit school and stay home and paint.

I want to have time to do all the things we <u>used</u> to do in school,
Without someone making me look like a fool.
I can't read those words,
I don't know what they say,
But I'll listen to you read to me any day.
Why do I have to sit in that group?
I'd rather be outside jumping through a hoop.
I used to like school when we'd have Share and Tell;
Now the teacher is too busy listening to bells.
"Next group," she says as she pulls out her hair;
I bet she'd rather be teaching us about squares.
Why do we have to learn to read?
I'd rather just be stringing beads.
That was fun and I was good.
Now school's a bore—and so is childhood!
We used to play with puppets, blocks, and sand;
Sometimes we even had a rhythm band!
Now school's a bore with nothing but books;
When the fire engine goes by, we can't even take time to look.
When the teacher says it's time to read,
I'd rather be planting flower seeds.
School used to be fun, but not anymore,
I even hate to walk through the door.
We used to pretend that we were ducks and elephants.
Now we have to look at our books while someone grunts.
Whoever decided that we should read books?
Don't they know we would rather be cooks?
I remember when we had so much fun making vegetable soup,
But now in our reading group the teacher calls us nincompoops.
She does not seem as happy anymore,
I bet she thinks that school is a bore.
Someday maybe I'll learn to read,
But right now I just want to succeed.
Maybe the teacher will come to her senses,
And realize we are not ready for pretenses.
Maybe the teacher will wake up someday,
And realize we are all in dismay.
Until then I'll just have to cry.
Because I can't read, as hard as I try.

We hope that none of your children will feel the frustrations expressed by this child, and so we have designed this book to provide you with the necessary assessments, materials, activities, and ideas to ensure success in beginning reading. Now that the different levels of perceptual skills have been defined, let us look at how to determine the needs of students and at ways of using the materials, activities, and ideas in this book.

ASSESSING THE PREREADING NEEDS OF STUDENTS

There are four different techniques to determine the prereading needs of students: observation, parent conferences or questionnaires, skills tests, and standardized tests.

The most common way to determine the prereading needs of students is to observe them in their typical work and play activities. You can use an Observation Guide for Prereading such as the one found in chapter 2 to guide your observations. When children are participating in some cutting and pasting activity, you can determine those children who are able to cut following a straight line. You can observe auditory skills as the children respond to tapes and records. During many of the play activities, you will notice children who can run, hop, and skip. Of course, these observations are only possible if you know the kinds of behaviors that are demonstrated at each level of performance for the prereading skills.

A second way of gathering information about the prereading needs of students is by talking with parents or by having them complete a questionnaire concerning their child. The parents of a young child usually are eager for their child to succeed in school and are willing to work cooperatively with you. They are also usually very well informed concerning the characteristics and achievements of their child; therefore, you shouldn't hesitate to use parents as a source of information. A Home Information Report, which you can have parents complete, is provided in chapter 2. You can use this Home Information Report as a guide for conducting parent-teacher conferences at school or when making home visits.

The third major way of determining the prereading needs of students is to use skills tests. In chapter 2, we provide directions for the skills tests for each level of performance for visual-motor coordination, auditory skills, and visual skills. In the Appendix, you can find the ready-to-reproduce skills tests to be handed out to the children. Skills tests for the other three major prereading areas—concept development, oral language, and readiness for books—can be found in *Getting Ready to Read: Book 2*. As you examine the skills tests provided in chapter 2, you will notice the skill being tested and the level of performance are indicated in the upper-left-hand corner. You have permission to remove the skills tests from the book, put them on thermofax masters, or prepare them in anyway you would like for use with your students.

Nearly all of the skills tests are designed for administration to small groups of children. We recommend not testing more than ten children at one time. Young children are frequently confused by directions, thus it is better to have a small group of children so you can make sure they all understand the directions. As you administer the skills tests, be sure the children understand such key concepts as "rhyme," "different," "sound alike at the beginning," and so forth.

We would encourage you to keep in mind that these skills tests are simply samples of behavior and you must combine the results with your information from daily observations to identify the specific prereading needs of each student. In fact, we would suggest you use the skills tests in this book after you have had an opportunity to observe the children for awhile. If you believe a child is on level two in a particular area, you can begin with the level two skills tests. It is not necessary to begin with the skills tests for level one and administer all three levels of tests to each child. You may even want to begin by administering a level three skills test if you believe—based on your observations—that a child might be performing at the third level for a particular skill.

The skills tests may also be given without regard to the sequence of the prereading skills presented in this book. For example, you may want to give some of the skills tests from the visual skills area first, and visual-motor coordination skills tests second. This is possible since children *gradually* develop in each of the prereading areas at the same time rather than developing skills in one area before moving on to the next area.

The fourth technique for determining the prereading needs of students is to use standardized tests. The last section of chapter 2 contains two lists of commonly used standardized tests. The first list presents selected survey tests that attempt to assess many different prereading needs. We have identified the subtests provided in these standardized tests so you can have an idea of what types of information you will obtain. The major advantage of such standardized tests is that norms are included, so you can compare your students with others. At the same time, you can get valuable diagnostic information if you analyze the results of the various subtests.

In addition to the list of reading readiness survey tests, we have included a list of tests that can be used to obtain specific information concerning each of the perceptual skills. If you desire more in-depth information about one area, these tests are particularly helpful. For example, if you would like to have more information about a child's auditory skills, you can administer the Auditory Discrimination Test by Joseph Wepman.

A third list of standardized tests, entitled "School Readiness Tests and Inventories," can be found in *Getting Ready to Read: Book 2*. The tests on this list are generally used as screening devices to see if children are ready for school. They can also be used to determine advanced placement or if a child should repeat kindergarten. These tests are important to teaching reading because many of the subtests deal with prereading skills.

The names and addresses of the publishers of all the standardized tests selected for our lists are found at the end of chapter 2. We suggest sending for a specimen set before ordering so you can select the tests that are most appropriate for your purposes.

We believe that by using these four assessment techniques you will be able to pinpoint the prereading needs of your students. Of course, young children change and grow rapidly in the different prereading areas so you must continually diagnose and notice their progress. Based on your assessments it is possible to predict when initial reading instruction is most likely to be successful. You also will find information in the manuals for standardized tests to guide your predictions and an index of reading readiness is provided in module 3 of *Developing Competencies in Teaching Reading* by Forgan and Mangrum (Charles Merrill, 1979).

A word of caution: If you do find a child who has demonstrated the prerequisites for reading, do not have the child participate in the readiness program. Some children "don't like school anymore" because they get bored when they already have developed the prereading skills. Consider the thoughts of this young child who is ready to read.

I'm Ready to Read

I'm ready to read!
Why doesn't someone take heed?
I am just about to burst!
Doesn't anybody know what I should do first?
Doesn't the teacher know
That I'm ready to go?
Why do we keep playing "I Spy"?
Making me circle all those letter i's?
I know this says "dad," and that says "bad";
Please let me read so I don't feel so sad.
I've listened and listened to all the sounds,
Also made all the circles nice and round.
I'm ready to read!
Why doesn't someone take heed?
I like to play jump the rope,
And yet I really hope
That someone will teach me words,
So I can read about birds.
The teacher says, "Draw and color a picture."
I say, "Let's read a recipe and make a mixture."
One thing I just have to mention
Is sometimes I feel like not paying attention.
I'm tired of circling pictures that are the same,
And playing the sound-alike game;
I'm ready to read!
Why doesn't someone take heed?
When I talk I say lots of words.
I wonder why no one has heard.
If only I could learn to read the words I speak,
I'd be able to read a sentence by next week.
My brother talks about learning words by sight;
He taught me four words in just one night.
Now I know the words the, an, is and one.
Gee, that was really lots of fun.
But now my brother is busy playing ball,
And he says he hasn't any time at all.
I'm ready to read!
Why doesn't someone take heed?

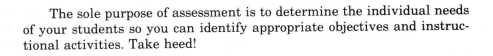

The sole purpose of assessment is to determine the individual needs of your students so you can identify appropriate objectives and instructional activities. Take heed!

KEEPING RECORDS OF PROGRESS

A "group profile of prereading needs" is provided at the end of chapter 2 to aid in keeping records of the different levels of performance of your children. The group record may be used to help identify children with common prereading needs. It will be especially valuable if you have small skills groups focussing on the different prereading skills and levels of performance, or if you set up learning centers in the classroom covering the different prereading areas. You can look at the group record and determine those students who should be attending a particular learning center and/or skills group. It is possible to set up a very well-equipped and exciting learning center for each of the prereading areas using the ready-to-make activities found in chapter 3 of this book and some of the commercial activities that are suggested in chapter 4.

An individual-record-keeping form is available in *Getting Ready to Read: Book 2*. The individual profile is provided for use in conducting parent-teacher conferences. In addition to helping you describe the strengths and weaknesses of a particular child, the profile is useful in helping parents understand the importance of reading readiness. Unfortunately, there are some parents who are eager to push their child into formal reading instruction without the necessary prerequisites. The individual profile of a child should be completed and shared with the parents who are applying pressure to "stop having Susie play, and teach her to read."

USING THE READY-TO-MAKE ACTIVITIES

The heart of this book—chapter 3—includes many ready-to-make activities for each level of performance for visual-motor coordination, auditory skills, and visual skills. Ready-to-make activities for concept development, oral language development, and readiness for books are available in *Getting Ready to Read: Book 2*. The activities include "folder" activities, "envelope" activities, and reproducible pages. The folder activities are those that are made from and stored in manila folders, whereas the envelope activities include materials that are best stored in envelopes.

Each activity includes "Directions for Making" and "Directions for Using." In preparing the activities for use, it is important to follow each step of the construction directions carefully. On the other hand, the directions for use can be adapted for the needs and abilities of your students.

The folder activities are inexpensive and easy to make. All of these activities have essentially three parts. First, on the front of each folder there is an attractive picture. Each of the pictures is provided in the Appendix. We suggest that you color them before adhering them to the front of the folders. You should also write the title of the activity on each folder. The inside of the folders contains the actual game board or materials for the activity. The patterns you will need for the materials found inside of the folders are also provided in the Appendix. In some cases it will be necessary to make additional copies of something by tracing or duplicating. For example, you need to trace twelve fish for the "Fishing for Shapes" activity provided for level two of visual-motor coordination. The third part of the folder, the back, contains the "Directions for Using" and, if needed, envelopes to store the materials necessary for the activity. If desired, the "Directions for Using" can simply be cut out of the book and glued on the back of the folders. These directions are designed to be read by the teacher or leader of the activity.

Some of the activities do not require folders, as the materials needed can be easily stored in large envelopes. The directions for preparing the materials for envelope activities are detailed and pictures are provided so you can decorate the front of the envelopes if desired.

Most of the activities can be made from the following materials:

1. Manila folders—We recommend using different colored folders for the different prereading areas. For example, you may want to use red for the visual-motor coordination, yellow for the auditory skills, and blue for the visual skills.

2. Magic Markers—These are for coloring the pictures to be placed on the folders or envelopes.

3. Tagboard or heavy poster board—This is used for making the parts for different activities.

4. Spinners or dice

5. Glue

6. Small envelopes—These are used to hold game or activity pieces.

7. Large envelopes

8. Tracing paper or access to a duplicating machine

9. Scissors

10. Laminating plastic or clear Con-Tact paper

In using some of the activities it also will be necessary to have tokens, crayons, and/or grease pencils available to the children.

We suggest getting parents or older elementary school students to help you in the preparation of the materials. We have found fourth-, fifth-, or sixth-grade students able to follow the directions and actually prepare the activities. In some school systems, parents are invited to attend a morning or evening workshop at which they make materials for the teachers. It is amazing how many different materials can be made by ten parents working for three hours.

The activities are designed to involve the children actively; thus, many of them have loose pieces that the children manipulate. These pieces should be placed in small envelopes, which are attached to the back of the folders. It is a good idea to number or color code each piece in some manner so the pieces for each activity can be kept together. For example, you may want to code the pieces to the activities by writing the number of the activity on the back of each piece. If you will write this code on the outside of the folder and envelope as well as on the loose pieces, you will be able to keep the activities and the materials together. Of course, it is important to teach the children to take care of these materials and to put the different parts back in the envelopes before going on to another activity.

Folders and other materials needed for the activities should be laminated to protect them from daily wear and tear. This can either be done by using clear Con-Tact paper, which is available in most discount and hardware stores, or by using a laminating machine, if one is available. Before laminating, it is very important that all labeling (including coding) has been done. After a folder is laminated, you can use a single-edge razor blade to make a slit in the back for the flap of the envelope containing the materials.

We would encourage you to adapt the materials in the activities to your own students. In some activities, pictures are required and we do provide these pictures for you. At the same time, you may want to adapt the activity by cutting additional pictures out of catalogs or old reading readiness workbooks. You can provide more variations of the activities by changing the numerals, letters, or other materials. Remember—you are the expert on your children!

When using the activities with children, select those activities that are appropriate to their prereading needs. It is not necessary for all children to begin with level one activities, and then proceed to level two, and finally level three. You should provide for the individual differences, based on the diagnostic information you obtained from observation, parents, skills tests, or standardized reading readiness tests.

Although they should work at their skill level most of the time, children may enjoy using some of the activities at a lower level. Children who are performing at level three should be allowed to use some of the level one or two activities just for fun or to feel "smart." Children do like to do things they can do well!

The activities within each of the three levels of performance are not sequenced according to difficulty. For example, there are four activities for level one of visual skills. All four of these activities are appropriate for children who are performing at level one. However, some activities within a level may be more difficult for some children.

Some of the activities require supervision. We have found that once you have introduced the activities to the children, and demonstrated the directions for using them, the children will be able to use most of them independently. However, as you guide the students in the use of the activities many teachable moments will occur. Take advantage of these times by actually showing the children how to do something. If you just provide the activities for independent use, you will miss many opportunities for helping children.

If you do want the children to use some of the activities independently, make the activities self-correcting by providing the answers. This can be done for activities such as "Feed the Bunnies," where words on carrots are matched to particular baskets with letters. Each basket can be marked with a particular color, and the carrots that fit into the basket marked on the back with the same color. Many teachers like to make self-correcting activities so children can get immediate feedback without interrupting the teacher. At the same time, we would encourage you to provide verbal praise and pats on the back as the children successfully use the activities. The relationships you develop with your students, not just the materials you use, make it possible for them to succeed!

USING THE ADDITIONAL IDEAS AND MATERIALS FOR PARENTS AND TEACHERS

The fourth chapter of this book provides you with lists of additional ideas and commercial materials for use at home or school. Suggestions are provided for each one of the three levels of performance for visual-motor coordination, auditory skills, and visual skills. The objective for each level is stated, followed by a list of six to ten additional ideas, plus a list of five or six relevant commercial materials. Additional ideas and commercial materials for use at home or school for concept development, oral language development, and readiness for books are available in *Getting Ready to Read: Book 2*.

These lists have been prepared to give teachers other ideas that can be used in helping students develop the prereading skills and also because it is not possible to make all of the materials needed to help children develop these prerequisites. The list can also be used to provide parents with ideas and suggested materials they can use with their children. We recommend you first read all of the lists of ideas and materials, putting a check in front of those you would like to use. Later you will be able to refer to the list to find particular ideas and materials. During parent-teacher conferences, you might want to have the suggestions handy to provide ideas and to suggest particular materials to parents who are willing to help their child. You have permission to duplicate these lists of additional ideas and materials for use with individual parents. The ideas can also be duplicated and used in parent workshops and during parent-orientation programs.

Many of these activites are games that children enjoy and play on their own. For example, most children have played the game of dropping clothespins into a milk bottle. We included these common enjoyable activities to give you an idea of the appropriateness of the activities for the development of prereading skills at particular levels.

The format of the lists of commercial materials includes the name of the material, the publisher's code, and a brief description of the material. At the end of chapter 4 is a list, by code, of the publishing companies and their addresses. We suggest you send for catalogs from different publishers. These catalogs have more detailed descriptions and the prices of the materials. Also, our list of commercial materials contains only a few of the many that are available; by obtaining the catalogs from the publishers, you will be able to make many additional selections.

SUMMARY

In summary, this book provides you with an Observation Guide for Prereading, a Home Information Report, skills tests that are ready for you to use to assess the needs of your students, and a list of standardized tests for further diagnosis and comparison. Ready-to-make activities for the three levels of the perceptual skills also are provided for your use. Finally, additional ideas and selected commercial materials are presented for the many different levels of development in the prereading areas.

We believe this is a book that is not going to sit on your shelf, but rather one that you will use! Duplicate the Observation Guide, Home Information Report, and skills tests for use with your students. Have fun making the activities with the help of others. Feel free to duplicate the additional ideas and materials for use with parents, or simply use this list as a source of ideas. Our hope is that you will enjoy using the materials and ideas in this book as much as we have enjoyed developing them. It is a pleasure to use the activities with children and observe how enthusiastic they are! The smiles on their faces, as well as the serious looks as they think, will make your efforts worthwhile!

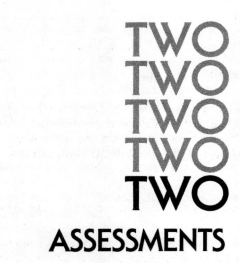

TWO

ASSESSMENTS

OBSERVATION GUIDE FOR PREREADING

Directions: As you observe a child in work and play activities, please note the behaviors that typically describe his or her performance for each of the prereading areas. Check the level of performance for each area. Review the more detailed descriptions in chapter 1 when in doubt.

Visual-Motor Coordination

—————— Level 1: Controls large muscles in running and hopping; scribbles with crayons, staying on the paper.

—————— Level 2: Can connect dots in a straight line when the dots are one inch apart; can reproduce a circle, square, and triangle; can turn pages of a book carefully.

—————— Level 3: Can copy most letters; cuts on a straight line using scissors; can stay within the lines when coloring big objects.

Auditory Skills

—————— Level 1: Distinguishes and remembers grossly different environmental sounds; reproduces simple rhythmic patterns.

—————— Level 2: Discriminates sounds in the initial positions of words; can repeat three unrelated words in sequence.

—————— Level 3: Discriminates rhyming words; can repeat four unrelated words in sequence.

Visual Skills

—————— Level 1: Discriminates and remembers grossly different geometric shapes such as circles, squares, and triangles.

—————— Level 2: Discriminates letter forms in isolation; can recognize own name.

—————— Level 3: Discriminates letters in words that are different in the initial, medial, or final positions. Is able to remember a sequence of three letters; thus, can recognize words.

HOME INFORMATION REPORT

Directions to Parents: I want to get to know your child as well as possible so I can do my best in helping him be successful in school. This form contains questions that would provide me with useful information concerning your child. I would like you to respond to those questions that you desire, and return this questionnaire with your child. If you want a parent-teacher conference to discuss your child, I will be most happy to meet with you.

1. Child's Name _____ Sex _____ Birthday _____

2. Address _____ Phone _____

3. Father's Name _____ Father's Occupation _____

4. Mother's Name _____ Mother's Occupation _____

5. Do parents live together? _____ If not, what is the marital status? _____

6. Who are the other children in your family and what are their ages? _____

   _____

   _____

7. Is a language other than English spoken at home? _____ If so, what? _____

8. Does your child seem to enjoy being read to by others? _____

   If so, by whom and for how long? _____

   _____

9. Does your child ask what different words say? _____

10. What types of books do you read to your child? _____

11. What are your child's favorite TV programs? _____

12. How long does your child spend in a typical day watching TV? _____

13. Has your child been to the public library within the last three months? _____

14. Has your child ever had any difficulty with ears or hearing? _____ If so, please

    describe. _____

    _____

15. Has your child ever had any problem with eyes or visual defects? _____ If so,

    please describe. _____

    _____

16. Does your child have any physical defects or health problems that might hinder progress and mobility in school? _____ If so, please describe. _____

_____

17. Does your child have playmates in the neighborhood? _____ If so, what are their

ages? _____

18. What are your child's favorite play activities? _____

19. What places has your child visited (example: zoo)? _____

_____

20. What other information can you provide to help me do a better job in teaching your child?

_____

21. Please list those questions you have about your child's school program.

_____

_____

SKILLS TEST 1   (Refer to the Appendix for reproducible materials)

Visual-Motor Coordination—Level 1

Directions to the Teacher: Give copies of Skills Test 1 to the children, provide crayons, and direct them to color the apple. The children should be able to color the apple staying on the paper and going no more than one inch outside of the lines of the apple. Use some of the level 1 activities with the children who cannot complete this task successfully.

SKILLS TEST 2

Visual-Motor Coordination—Level 2

Directions to the Teacher: Provide each child with a copy of Skills Test 2. Tell the children to look at the first part of the skills test and to make a shape like the one in each box. For example, tell them to make a circle just like the one that is in the first box. When they have completed their reproductions, ask them to draw a line to connect the dots to get the dog to the bone. Tell them to be careful so they connect each dot. In evaluating the responses of the children notice if:

     a. The circle is essentially round and closed.
     b. The square is more like a box than a circle. Three of the four corners should meet even if they are not right angles.
     c. The triangle has a base line and corners.
     d. The line connecting the dots touches all but one of the dots and is essentially straight.

Provide level two activities for the children who cannot complete three of these four tasks successfully.

SKILLS TEST 3

Visual-Motor Coordination—Level 3 (Upper-Case Letters)

Directions to the Teacher: Provide each child with a copy of Skills Test 3 and tell the children you want to see how well they are learning to make their upper-case letters. Tell the children to make a letter just like the one you have made in each box. Point out the guidelines to the children. In evaluating the papers of the children, see which letters are causing difficulty and then use or adapt some of the visual-motor activities for level 3.

SKILLS TEST 4

Visual-Motor Coordination—Level 3 (Lower-Case Letters)

Directions to the Teacher: Provide the children with a copy of Skills Test 4 and tell them you want to see how well they are learning to make their lower-case letters. Tell the children to make a letter just like the one you have made in each box. Point out the guidelines to the children. In evaluating the papers of the children, see which letters are causing difficulty and then use or adapt some of the visual-motor activities for level 3.

SKILLS TEST 5

Auditory Skills—Level 1 (Discrimination)

Directions to the Teacher: Give each child a copy of Skills Test 5 and tell the children you are going to make some sounds. Ask them to circle the thing in each row that makes the sound you make. For example, direct the children to first look at the star row. Now make the sound of a dog and ask them to circle the picture that makes the sound you made. Make sure the children understand the directions and then proceed. Make the following sounds: siren, telephone, cat, and bird for each row in sequence.

As you observe the children and evaluate their responses see which environmental sounds they are having a hard time discriminating or remembering. Use or adapt some of the level 1 activities for children who do not get all items correct.

SKILLS TEST 6

Auditory Skills—Level 1 (Memory)

Directions to the Teacher: Tell the children you are going to see how well they can listen and follow your directions. Give each child a copy of Skills Test 6 and have the children notice the three separate boxes. Tell them you are going to ask them to draw a line in each box from one thing to another. You will tell them only one time what to do. They must listen carefully and try to remember what to do. They cannot begin drawing the lines until you say "go." Read the directions at a normal rate of reading, and say "go" after each set of directions. For example, direct the children's attention to the first box. Have them name the three objects in the box (house, book, and cat). Then ask the children to put their pencils on the house and draw a line from the house to the cat, and from the cat to the book. Say "go," and do not repeat the direction. Now direct the children's attention to the sock box. Have them put their pencils on the duck. Tell the children to draw a line from the duck to the clock, and from the clock to the tree. Now direct the children's attention to the ball box. Have the children put their pencils on the dog. Tell them to draw a line from the dog to the bed, and from the bed to the umbrella. The children should be able to draw all three lines correctly. If a child has difficulty, use some of the auditory-memory activities for level 1.

SKILLS TEST 7

Auditory Skills—Level 2 (Discrimination)

Directions to the Teacher: Give a copy of Skills Test 7 to each child. Tell the children to look at the three objects in each row and then cross out the one that does not sound like the others at the beginning. Do the first one together to make sure the children understand what is meant by beginning sounds. As you evaluate the children's responses see which sounds they are having a difficult time discriminating. Use or adapt some of the level 2 activities with children who do not get all items correct.

SKILLS TEST 8

Auditory Skills—Level 2 (Memory)

Directions to the Teacher: Tell the children you are going to give them some directions to follow. They will have to listen carefully to you so they will know what to do. Give each child a copy of Skills Test 8 and have the children notice the three separate boxes. Tell them you are going to have them draw lines from one picture to another in each box. They cannot begin drawing the lines until you say "go." You should read the directions at a normal rate of reading and say "go" after each set of directions. For example, have them find box 1 and point out the four objects in the box (apple, house, book, and dog). Then direct the children to put their pencils on the apple. Ask them to draw a line from the apple to the dog, from the dog to the book, and from the book to the house. For box 2, ask them to put their pencils on the hammer. Ask them to draw a line from the hammer to the key, from the key to the clock, and from the clock to the duck. For box 3, ask them to put their pencils on the cat. Ask them to draw a line from the cat to the car, from the car to the banana, and from the banana to the tree. The children should get all of these objects correct. If a child misses any of the items use some of the level 2 activities for auditory memory.

SKILLS TEST 9

Auditory Skills—Level 3 (Discrimination)

Directions to the Teacher: Give a copy of Skills Test 9 to each child. Tell the children there are three pictures in each row. Two of the words rhyme and one does not. The children should cross out the one that does not rhyme. Do the first row together to make sure the children understand what is meant by "rhyme." As you evaluate the children's responses, see which sound patterns they are having a hard time discriminating. Use or adapt some of the level 3 activities for the children who do not get all items correct.

SKILLS TEST 10

Auditory Skills—Level 3 (Memory)

Directions to the Teacher: Tell the children you are going to see how carefully they can listen to your directions. Give each child a copy of Skills Test 10. Tell them you will ask them to draw a line from one thing to another, and they must listen carefully and remember where to draw their lines. They cannot begin drawing the lines until you say "go." You should read the directions at a normal rate of reading, and say "go" after each set of directions. They should listen to you carefully as you will not repeat what you say. For example, direct the children's attention to box 1. Have the children name the objects in the box (apple, book, car, dog, and house). Then tell the children to put their pencils on the apple in box 1, and ask them to draw a line from the apple to the house, from the house to the book, from the book to the car, and from the car to the dog. For box 2, direct the children to put their pencils on the clock. Ask the children to draw a line from the clock to the cat, from the cat to the tree, from the tree to the ball, and from the ball to the car. For box 3, tell the children to put their pencils on the picture of the rake and draw a line from the rake to the orange, from the orange to the flower, from the flower to the boy, and from the boy to the fish. The children should be able to get all of the objects correct. If they do not, use some of the auditory-memory activities for level 3.

SKILLS TEST 11

Visual Skills—Level 1 (Discrimination)

Directions to the Teacher: Provide each child with a copy of Skills Test 11. Tell them to look at the shapes in each row and direct them to put an X over the one that is different from the others. The children should get all of the items correct. If the children miss an item, use some of the visual-discrimination activities for level 1.

SKILLS TEST 12

Visual Skills—Level 1 (Memory)

Directions to the Teacher: Duplicate a copy of Skills Test 12 for each child. You will also need to prepare three 5″ × 8″ index cards. Draw the shape of a circle on one card, a square on another, and a triangle on the third. Distribute the papers to the children face down. Tell them you are going to show them a shape; then show the square. After they have had a chance to see it for five seconds, remove it from their sight, wait five seconds, and tell them to turn their papers over. Ask them to find the umbrella row and put an X over the shape you showed them. Do the first one together to make sure the children understand the directions. Proceed in a similar manner by showing them the shape of the circle, then the triangle, and finally the square again. The children should be able to get all of these items correct. If a child misses an item, use some of the visual-memory activities for level 1.

SKILLS TEST 13

Visual Skills—Level 2 (Discrimination)

Directions to the Teacher: Give a copy of Skills Test 13 to each child. Direct the children to find row 1. Tell them to look at each letter in the row and put an X over the one that is different. Have them complete the page independently. As you evaluate the responses, notice which letters the children are having a difficult time discriminating. If a child misses any of the items, use the visual-discrimination activities for level 2.

SKILLS TEST 14

Visual Skills—Level 2 (Memory)

Directions to the Teacher: You will need to duplicate a copy of Skills Test 14 for each child, and prepare five 5" × 8" cards, one for each one of the following letters: S, T, A, C, and B. Distribute the papers face down. Tell the children you are going to show them one letter, and when you take it away, you will ask them to turn their papers over and mark the letter in the first row that you showed them. Begin by showing the children the letter C. Expose it for five seconds, wait five seconds, and ask them to turn their papers over and find row 1. They should now put an X over the letter you showed them. Repeat this procedure in a similar manner for the remaining rows, showing the letters A, T, B, and S. Children should get all of these items correct. If they miss one item, use some of the visual-memory activities for level 2.

SKILLS TEST 15

Visual Skills—Level 3 (Discrimination)

Directions to the Teacher: Provide each child with a copy of Skills Test 15. Ask them to find row 1. Tell them they are to look at each word in row 1, and cross out the one that is different. Allow the children to complete the page independently. You will notice the first four items include words that are different at the beginning only, the next four items words that are different at the end, and the last four items words that are different in the medial position. Note if the children make errors in discriminating words at the beginning, final, or medial positions. If the children miss any of the items, use some of the visual-discrimination activities for level 3.

SKILLS TEST 16

Visual Skills—Level 3 (Memory)

Directions to the Teacher: Duplicate a copy of Skills Test 16 for each child. In addition, make four 5″ × 8″ cards, one with each of the following letter combinations: tba, bat, tab, and bta. Distribute the papers face down and tell the children you are going to show them a card with letters on it and then take it away. After you take it away, you are going to ask them to turn their papers over and find one just like yours. Begin by showing the children tab. Expose it for five seconds, remove it from their sight, and wait five seconds. Ask the children to turn their papers over and mark the word they saw in row 1. Continue the same procedures for row 2 using bat, row 3 exposing tba, and row 4 exposing bta. The children should get all of the items correct. If not, use some of the visual-memory activities for level 3.

GROUP PROFILE OF PREREADING NEEDS

STUDENT'S NAME	VISUAL-MOTOR COORDINATION			AUDITORY SKILLS			VISUAL SKILLS			CONCEPT DEVELOPMENT			ORAL LANGUAGE			READINESS FOR BOOKS		
Levels	1	2	3	1	2	3	1	2	3	1	2	3	1	2	3	1	2	3
1.																		
2.																		
3.																		
4.																		
5.																		
6.																		
7.																		
8.																		
9.																		
10.																		
11.																		
12.																		
13.																		
14.																		
15.																		
16.																		
17.																		
18.																		
19.																		
20.																		

A. GENERAL STANDARDIZED READING READINESS TESTS

1. Clymer-Barrett Prereading Battery

This test consists of a diagnostic battery which yields scores for the following: Visual discrimination, auditory discrimination, and visual-motor skills. A checklist of readiness behaviors is also included. Time: 50 minutes. Authors are Clymer and Barrett. Available from Personnel Press, Inc.

2. Gates-MacGinitie Readiness Skills Test

This test includes eight subtests but only the following seven subtests are combined to get a total readiness score: Listening Comprehension, Auditory Discrimination, Visual Discrimination, Following Directions, Letter Recognition, Visual-Motor Coordination, and Word Recognition. Time: 120 minutes. Authors are Gates and MacGinitie. Available from Teachers' College Press, Columbia University.

3. Harrison-Stroud Reading Readiness Profile

This test includes six subtests. The first five can be administered on a group basis, but the sixth subtest must be administered individually. The subtests included are Using Symbols, Making Visual Discriminations, Using the Context, Making Auditory Discrimination, Using Context and Auditory Clues, and Giving the Names of the Letters. Time: 80 minutes. Authors are Harrison and Stroud. Available from Houghton Mifflin Company.

4. Lee-Clark Reading Readiness Test

This test is composed of three parts made up of four subtests as follows: Part I concerns Letter Symbols, Part II covers Concepts, and Part III covers Word Symbols. Time: 20 minutes. Authors are Lee and Clark. Available from California Test Bureau.

5. Macmillan Reading Readiness Test

This test includes the following subtests; Qualified Rating Scale, Visual Discrimination, Auditory Discrimination, Vocabulary and Concepts, Letter Names, Visual Motor. Time: 75–90 minutes (three to five sessions). Authors are Harris and Sipay. Available from Macmillan Company.

6. Metropolitan Readiness Test

This test includes two levels. The first half of kindergarten (level 1) includes the following subtests: Auditory Memory, Rhyming, Visual Skills (Letter Recognition, Visual Matching, Total) and Language Skills (School Language Listening, Quantitative Language, Total). The level 2 test is used for the second half of kindergarten and in first grade. The subtests are: Auditory Skills, Visual Skills, Language Skills, Quantitative Skills, and Copying. Time: Level 1 requires 105 minutes (seven sessions) and levels 2 takes 110 minutes (five sessions). Authors are Nurss and McGauvran. Available from Psychological Corporation.

7. Murphy-Durrell Reading Readiness Analysis

This test consists of the following three subtests: Phonemes, Letter Names, and Learning Rate. Time: 60 minutes (two sessions). Authors are Murphy and Durrell. Available from Psychological Corporation.

8. **PMA Readiness Level**

This test includes the following subtests: Auditory Discrimination, Verbal Meaning, Perceptual Speed, Number Facility, and Spatial Relations. Time: 60 minutes. The author is Thurstone. Available from Science Research Associates, Inc.

9. **Prereading Expectancy Screen Scales**

This test includes four subtests: Visual Sequencing, Visual/Auditory Spatial, Auditory Sequencing, and Letter Identification. Time: 25–35 minutes. Authors are Hartlage and Lucus. Available from Psychologists and Educators, Inc.

10. **Reading Aptitude Tests**

This test includes the following seven subtests: Motor Coordination, Perception of Forms, Visual Memory for Forms, Auditory Discrimination, Maze Tracing, Blending of Sounds, and Auditory Vocabulary. In addition, individual subtests of articulation, auditory memory of a story, and name writing are used. Time: Parts 1–2 require about 60 minutes. Part 3 takes about 35–50 minutes. The author is Monroe. Available from Houghton Mifflin Company.

B. SPECIALIZED TESTS FOR PARTICULAR PREREADING AREAS

Visual-Motor Coordination

1. **Bruininks-Oseretsky Test of Motor Proficiency**

This test is an individual, wide-range test of motor development which includes the following eight subtests: Running Speed and Agility, Balance, Bilateral Coordination, Strength, Upper-Limb Coordination, Response Speed, Visual-Motor Control, and Upper-Limb Speed and Dexterity. Time: 45–60 minutes. The author is Bruininks. Available from American Guidance Services.

2. **Frostig Movement Skills Test Battery**

This test includes six summary scores: Hand-Eye Coordination, Strength, Balance, Visually Guided Movement, Flexibility, Total. Time: 20–25 minutes. The author is Orpet. Available from Consulting Psychologists Press, Inc.

3. **Primary Visual Motor Test**

This test includes sixteen geometric designs to be copied by the child. Time: 10–20 minutes. The author is Haworth. Available from Grune and Stratton, Inc.

Auditory Discrimination Tests

1. **Auditory Discrimination Test**

This quickly administered test assesses a child's ability to recognize the fine differences that exist between the phonemes used in English speech. Time: 5–10 minutes. The author is Wepman. The test is available from Language Research Associates, Inc.

2. **Goldman-Fristoe-Woodcock Auditory Skills Test Battery**

This test consists of a comprehensive battery of tests for diagnostic assessment of auditory skills. Time: 10–15 minutes. Authors are Goldman, Fristoe, and Woodcock. Available from American Guidance Services.

3. Lindamood Auditory Conceptualization Test

This easily administered test provides a measure of a student's level of auditory functioning in two areas: (1) the ability to discriminate one speech sound from another, and (2) the ability to perceive the number, order, and sameness or difference of speech sounds in sequences. Time: 10–35 minutes. Authors are Lindamood and Lindamood. Available from Teaching Resources Corporation.

Visual Perception Tests

1. Marianne Frostig Development Test of Visual Perception

Test includes seven scores: Eye-Motor Coordination, Figure Ground Discrimination, Form Constancy, Position in Space, Spatial Relations, Total, and Perceptual Quotient. Time: 40–60 minutes. Authors are Lefever, Whittlesey, Maslow. Available from consulting Psychologists Press, Inc.

2. Motor-Free Visual Perception Test

This test is a quick measure of overall visual-perceptual processing ability in children. It is a thirty-six item test. Time: 10 minutes. The authors are Colarusso and Hammill. Available from Academic Therapy Publishers.

ADDRESSES OF TEST PUBLISHERS

Academic Therapy Publishers
1539 Fourth Street
San Rafael, CA 94901

American Guidance Services
Publishers' Building
Circle Pines, MN 55014

California Test Bureau
McGraw-Hill Book Co., Inc.
1221 Avenue of the Americas
New York, NY 10020

Consulting Psychologists Press, Inc.
577 College Avenue
Palo Alto, CA 94306

Grune and Stratton, Inc.
111 Fifth Avenue
New York, NY 10003

Houghton Mifflin Company
1 Beacon Street
Boston, MA 02107

Macmillan Company
866 Third Avenue
New York, NY 10022

Language Research Associates, Inc.
175 East Delaware Place
Chicago, IL 60611

Personnel Press Inc.
20 Nassau St.
Princeton, NJ 08540

Psychological Corporation
757 Third Avenue
New York, NY 10017

Psychologists and Educators, Inc.
Suite 212, 211 West State Street
Jacksonville, IL 62650

Science Research Associates, Inc.
155 North Walker Drive
Chicago, IL 60606

Teachers' College Press
Columbia University
1234 Amsterdam Avenue
New York, NY 10027

Teaching Resources Corporation
100 Boylston Street
Boston, MA 02116

READY-TO-MAKE ACTIVITIES

(Refer to the Appendix for reproducible materials)

ACTIVITY 1

Visual-Motor Coordination—Level 1

Creepy Creatures

Fig. 1

Directions for Making

1. Trace or duplicate the shapes for Activity 1 so you have three sets.
2. Adhere the sets of shapes to tagboard, color code sets to keep them separate, laminate, and cut out. Put each set of shapes in a separate small envelope.
3. Decorate a large envelope by using shapes to draw a creature on front of the envelope. Label envelope (Fig. 1). Place the three smaller envelopes into the larger envelope.

Directions for Using

1. One to three children can use this activity.
2. Each child is given a set of shapes, a large (18″ × 24″) sheet of paper, and a pencil or crayon.
3. Tell the children to use some or all of these shapes to trace around and make a "Creepy Creature." After drawing the creature, the children may want to color it.
4. Allow the children to share their pictures if they want to do so.

ACTIVITY 2

Visual-Motor Coordination—Level 1

Hippity Hop

Directions for Making

1. Cut out and color the large foot for Activity 2, adhere it to the front of a folder for decoration, and label (Fig. 1).
2. Inside the folder, label one side "Team One" and the other side "Team Two." Using one of the footprint direction cards, trace four footsteps on each side (Fig. 2).
3. Trace or duplicate the footprint direction cards for Activity 2. Complete the directions on the cards to indicate specific places to which a child might hop, run, or jump. Adhere direction cards to tagboard, laminate, and cut out. Place cards in an envelope on the back of the folder (Fig. 3).
4. Laminate the folder.

Fig. 1

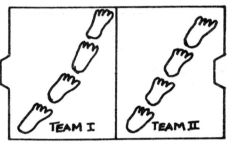

Fig. 2

Fig. 3

Directions for Using

1. Two teams can play this game with supervision.
2. Each team chooses a footprint path inside the folder.
3. The leader or teacher draws a footprint direction card and reads the directions.
4. The first player is asked to follow those directions. The teacher may want to indicate right or left so the children can learn these distinctions. If the child accomplishes the directions on the card, the footprint card is placed on the team's footprint outline inside the folder. If the first player cannot accomplish the task on card, the next player on the other team may try.
5. Game continues until one team has all footprint outlines in folder completed.

ACTIVITY 3

Visual-Motor Coordination—Level 1

Guess Who I Am!

Fig. 1

Directions for Making

1. Cut out and color the set of animal playing cards for Activity 3. Adhere to tagboard, laminate, and cut apart.
2. Trace and color several animal pictures from the cards, adhere to the front of an envelope for decoration, and label (Fig. 1).
3. Put animal cards in envelope.

Directions for Using

1. Two to four players can play this game with supervision.
2. Place animal playing cards facedown.
3. The first player draws a card, looks at the picture, and acts out the movement of the animal pictured.
4. Players try to guess the animal being acted out. The player who guesses the correct animal first gets the card and has the next turn for drawing a card and acting it out.

ACTIVITY 4

Visual-Motor Coordination—Level 2

Lace Me Up!

Fig. 1

Directions for Making

1. Cut out and color the three pages with large pictures for Activity 4. Adhere to tagboard and laminate.
2. Using a paper punch, punch holes where dots are indicated.
3. Duplicate one of the large pictures, color it, adhere it to the front of a large envelope for decoration, and label (Fig. 1).
4. Put lacing cards in envelope.

Directions for Using

1. This is an individual activity.
2. Give the child a lacing picture and a forty-inch shoelace with a knot at one end.
3. Tell the child to use the shoelace to go in and out of the holes.
4. When the activity is finished, the child may share the picture.
5. Child can remove shoelace and use it to lace the other pictures provided.

ACTIVITY 5

Visual-Motor Coordination—Level 2

Crazy Shapes

Fig. 1

Directions for Making

1. Trace or duplicate cards for Activity 5 so you have five sets: five cards with circles, five cards with triangles, five cards with squares, and five blank cards.
2. Adhere sets of cards to tagboard, laminate, and cut apart.
3. Decorate an envelope by drawing geometric shapes on it and label (Fig. 1).
4. Put the cards in the envelope.

Directions for Using

1. Two to four players can play this game with supervision.
2. Each player is given a grease pencil.
3. The teacher deals out four cards to each player and puts remaining cards in a pile facedown except for one. One card is turned faceup.
4. The first player looks at the faceup card. If the player has a card that matches the geometric shape, the matching card is placed over the faceup card.
5. If the card that is turned over is blank, the player may draw (using a grease pencil) a geometric shape on the blank card that matches a card in the player's hand and then place the matching card on the faceup card.
6. If the faceup card has a geometric shape on it and the player cannot match it, but the player has a blank card, the player may draw the geometric shape on the blank card to match it and play that card.
7. If a player cannot make a match, the player must draw one card from the facedown pile. If the player draws a match, the player may play the card on the faceup card. Otherwise, the player keeps the card in his hand and it is the next player's turn to attempt to match the faceup card.
8. Once the faceup card has been matched, the player who matches it takes the pair and places it in front of him. A new card is turned faceup.
9. Play continues from player to player in a clockwise manner, and the first player to run out of cards is the winner.

ACTIVITY 6

Visual-Motor Coordination—Level 2

Dashing with Dots to Monsterville

Directions for Making

1. Cut out and color the monster picture for Activity 6, adhere it to the front of a folder for decoration, and label (Fig. 1).
2. Cut out and color the paths and Monsterville for Activity 6. Adhere them to the inside of the folder (Fig. 2).
3. Adhere the pages of dot pictures for Activity 6 to tagboard, laminate, and cut apart. Place these in an envelope on the back of the folder (Fig. 3).
4. Laminate the folder.

Fig. 1

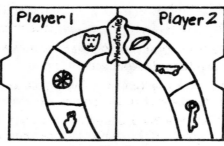
Fig. 2

Fig. 3

Directions for Using

1. Two players can play this game with supervision.
2. Each player is given a grease pencil, four tokens, and a paper towel.
3. Each player chooses a path to Monsterville inside the folder.
4. Dot picture cards are placed in a pile facedown. The teacher indicates to players that the line on the bottom of each picture indicates the bottom of picture and that they should begin drawing at the large black dot and follow the arrows.
5. Each player takes a dot picture card from the pile. Using a grease pencil, each player draws around the dots.
6. When finished with the picture, the player looks to see if that picture appears on the player's path. If it does, the player places a token on that picture. If the picture does not match, the player wipes the picture off and places it at the bottom of the dot picture pile.
7. Each player continues to do dot pictures and putting tokens on the pictures until one player has found a match for all of the pictures on his or her path. When all of the pictures are matched, the player places a token in Monsterville and is the winner.

ACTIVITY 7

Visual-Motor Coordination—Level 2

Fishing for Shapes

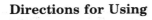

Fig. 1

Directions for Making

1. Trace or duplicate fish for Activity 7 so you have four of each fish. Adhere to tagboard, laminate, and cut out.
2. Attach a paper clip or magnetic tape to each fish.
3. Make a fishing pole by using a yardstick or tree twig. Attach a piece of yarn or string (approximately twenty-four inches long) to the pole. Tie a magnet or piece of magnetic tape to the end of the string.
4. Decorate an envelope by drawing a fish and labeling it (Fig. 1).
5. Put the fish in the envelope.

Directions for Using

1. Two to four players can play this game with supervision.
2. Each player is given a sheet of paper and a crayon or pencil.
3. The fish are turned facedown.
4. The first player is given the fishing pole and tries to catch a fish by touching the magnet to the paper clip.
5. When a fish has been caught, the player looks at the geometric shape on the fish. If the player can reproduce this shape on another sheet of paper the player gets to keep the fish. It is then the next player's turn.
6. The player with the most fish when all fish are used is the winner.

ACTIVITY 8

Visual-Motor Coordination—Level 3

And We're Off!

Directions for Making

1. Label and decorate the front of a folder (Fig. 1).
2. Trace or duplicate two copies of the maze for Activity 8. Adhere these mazes to the inside of the folder (Fig. 2).
3. Attach an envelope to hold grease pencils to the back of the folder (Fig. 3).
4. Laminate the folder.

Directions for Using

1. Two players can play this game.
2. Each player is given a grease pencil.

3. Tell the two players to draw a line from Tony's home to the toy store without crossing or touching the existing lines.

4. The first player to reach the toy store without crossing or touching the lines is the winner. Any path may be used unless you or the children designate a particular one.

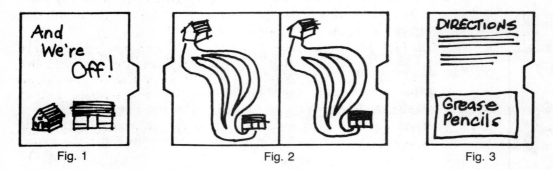

Fig. 1   Fig. 2   Fig. 3

ACTIVITY 9

Visual-Motor Coordination—Level 3

Color Me

Directions for Making

1. Cut out and color the large egg for Activity 9, adhere it to the front of a folder for decoration, and label (Fig. 1).

2. Using the large egg-coloring patterns for Activity 9, prepare a ditto master of each egg. Duplicate as many copies as needed (one for each child who will be doing the activity). Color the dots in each section of each egg as indicated. Put these egg-coloring papers in a large envelope and secure it to the folder with a large paper clip.

3. Label one side of the inside of the folder "Player 1" and label the other side "Player 2." Make dots approximately one and one-half inch apart up both sides of the folder (Fig. 2).

4. Trace or duplicate small egg pattern for Activity 9 so you have twelve eggs. Put colored dots in each of the eggs as follows: two eggs with green dots, two eggs with red dots, two eggs with blue dots, two eggs with black dots, two eggs with orange dots, and two eggs with yellow dots. Adhere to tagboard, laminate, and cut out. Separate these into two sets so you have one of each color egg in each set. Place each set in an envelope on the back of the folder (Fig. 3).

5. Laminate the folder.

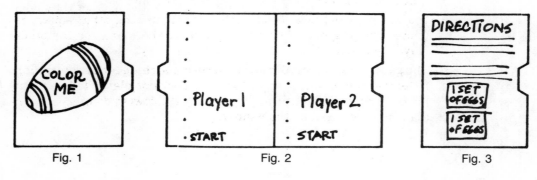

Fig. 1   Fig. 2   Fig. 3

Directions for Using

1. Two players can play this game with supervision.
2. Each player selects a side of the folder.
3. Each player is given an egg-coloring paper and crayons.
4. The teacher takes the two sets of small eggs and puts one egg face-down beside each dot on each side of folder (making sure there is one egg with dots of each color represented).
5. The first player uses a grease pencil and draws a line from the start dot to the first dot with an egg beside it, turns the egg over, and looks at the color of dots on the egg. If the color of dots matches one of the colored dots on the egg-coloring paper, the child colors in that segment. If not, it is the next player's turn.
6. Game continues until one player has completely colored an egg-coloring paper.

ACTIVITY 10

Visual-Motor Coordination—Level 3

Letter Dominoes

Directions for Making

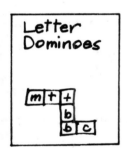

1. Adhere the pages of domino cards for Activity 10 to tagboard; laminate, cut out by following bold lines. (Each card will contain two letters.)
2. Trace three domino cards on the front of an envelope for decoration and label (Fig. 1).
3. Put all the cards into the envelope.

Directions for Using

1. Two to four players can play this game.
2. Each player is given a grease pencil.
3. A domino card with two letters on it is selected to start the game. The remainder of the dominoes are placed facedown.
4. Each player draws four dominoes. In order to play, the first player must have a letter to match one of the letters on the starter domino or, if the player has a blank square, the player may write in a letter to match a letter on the starter domino. If the player does not have a match, the player must draw dominoes until a match is found. (The matching card is placed as in regular dominoes.)
5. If a player matches a letter with a letter and the other square is blank, that player must write a letter on the blank for the other player to match.
6. The game continues with players in turn matching letters or writing letters on the blanks that will match. The first player to use all of his or her dominoes, or the player with the fewest dominoes when the pile is depleted, is the winner.

ACTIVITY 11

Auditory Skills—Level 1 (Memory)

Indian Signals

Directions for Making

1. Cut out and color Indian and smoke signals for Activity 11, adhere them to the front of a folder for decoration, and label (Fig. 1).
2. Trace or duplicate two Indian heads for Activity 11. Cut out and color the two Indian heads and adhere to the inside of the folder (Fig. 2).
3. Trace or duplicate twelve feathers using the pattern for Activity 11. Adhere to tagboard, laminate, and cut out. Put the feathers in an envelope on the back of the folder (Fig. 3).
4. Adhere the set of clapping-tapping cards for Activity 11 to tagboard, laminate, and cut apart. Put in another envelope on the back of the folder (Fig. 3).
5. Laminate the folder.

Fig. 1

Fig. 2

Fig. 3

Directions for Using

1. Two players can play this game with supervision.
2. Each player chooses an Indian head inside the folder and is given six feathers and a pencil or stick for tapping.
3. Clapping-tapping cards are shuffled and placed facedown.
4. The teacher draws a card. Using hands or a pencil, the teacher claps or taps the pattern on the card for the first player (the lines on the cards indicate a pause). The card is placed at the bottom of the pile after pattern has been tapped or clapped.
5. The first player is asked to reproduce the tapping pattern. If the pattern is repeated correctly, the player may choose a feather to put in the Indian's headdress.
6. Players take turns reproducing the patterns and the first player to complete the Indian's headdress is the winner.

ACTIVITY 12

Auditory Skills—Level 1 (Discrimination)

Animal Sounds

Directions for Making

1. Duplicate two sets of animal cards for Activity 12.
2. Color and cut out the animals on one set of cards and adhere to the front of an envelope for decoration; label the envelope (Fig. 1).
3. Color the second set of animal cards. Adhere to tagboard, laminate, and cut apart.
4. Put the animal cards in the envelope.

Directions for Using

1. Two to four players can play this game.
2. Animal cards are shuffled and placed facedown.
3. The first player draws a card, looks at the animal, and imitates the sound that animal makes.
4. Other players listen to the sound and try to guess what animal the sound represents.
5. The first player to guess the correct animal sound gets to keep the animal card, draws the next card, and imitates the sound the animal makes.
6. The player with the most animal cards at the end of the game is the winner.

ACTIVITY 13

Auditory Skills—Level 2 (Discrimination)

Let's Build a Car

Directions for Making

1. Trace or duplicate car for Activity 13 so you have three cars.
2. Cut out and color one car, adhere it to the front of a folder for decoration, and label (Fig. 1).
3. Cut out and color the other two cars and adhere them to the inside of the folder (Fig. 2).
4. Trace or duplicate a set of car parts for Activity 13. Color these parts and adhere to tagboard. Color the back of one set of parts red, and the back of the other set green (in order to keep the pieces separated). Laminate and cut apart. Place parts in an envelope on the back of the folder (Fig. 3).
5. Adhere the set of picture cards for Activity 13 to tagboard, laminate, and cut apart. Place cards in an envelope on the back of the folder (Fig. 3).
6. Laminate the folder.

Fig. 1

Fig. 2

Fig. 3

Directions for Using

1. Two players can play this game.
2. Each child chooses a car inside the folder and is given a set of car parts.
3. The picture cards are placed facedown. The first player draws a card and says the names of the two pictures on the card. The other player is directed to listen to see if the words pronounced are <u>exactly</u> the same.
4. After the second player responds yes or no, the card is shown to this player. If the words said were exactly the same, the card will have two pictures that are alike on it.
5. If the player responded correctly about the two words, the player may choose a car part to fill in the car.
6. The players take turns reading and responding to the cards, and the first player to fill in all the car parts is the winner.

ACTIVITY 14

Auditory Skills—Level 2 (Discrimination)

Otto the Octopus

Directions for Making

1. Cut out and color the plain octopus for Activity 14, adhere it to the front of the folder for decoration, and label (Fig. 1).
2. Cut out and color the two decorated octopi for Activity 14 and adhere them to the inside of the folder (Fig. 2).
3. Adhere the set of picture cards for Activity 14 to tagboard, laminate, and cut apart. Put the picture cards in an envelope on the back of the folder (Fig. 3).
4. Laminate the folder.

Directions for Using

1. Two players can play this game, with another child as the leader.
2. Each player is given eight tokens or a grease pencil and chooses one of the octopi inside the folder.
3. Picture cards are placed facedown.

4. A child, other than the two players, turns a picture card over and says the word for the picture. Both players listen carefully to the word. If the word begins with the same sound as the word for any of the pictures on the tentacles of the player's octopus, the player places a token on that picture or marks an X on it with the grease pencil.

5. The player who has the most tentacles covered or marked when all the cards are used is the winner.

Fig. 1

Fig. 2

Fig. 3

ACTIVITY 15

Auditory Skills—Level 2 (Memory)

Pete the Repeat

Directions for Making

1. Label and decorate the front of a folder (Fig. 1).
2. Cut and color game board for Activity 15. Adhere to the inside of the folder (Fig. 2).
3. Adhere the set of picture cards for Activity 15 to tagboard. Color, laminate, and cut apart. Place in an envelope on the back of the folder (Fig. 3).
4. Laminate the folder.

Fig. 1

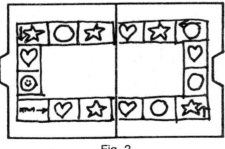

Fig. 2

Fig. 3

Directions for Using

1. Two to four players can play this game.
2. Each player is given a token.
3. Picture cards are placed facedown in a pile.

4. One child draws a card, without other players seeing the card, and says the names for the pictures on card.

5. The first player on the child's right is asked to repeat the names of the pictures in order. If the three words are repeated correctly, the player may move his or her token to the next symbol on the game board that matches the symbol on the top of the picture card. This player then draws a picture card and says the names of the pictures for the next player to the right to repeat.

6. Caution players to say the words slowly and to repeat the words only one time. If a child cannot repeat the words, it is the next player's turn.

7. Once a player has reached the last circle, star, or heart symbol on the gameboard, the next word card that player gets correct puts him or her into the winner section and wins the game.

ACTIVITY 16

Auditory Skills—Level 2 (Discrimination)

Smiley Face

Fig. 1

Directions for Making

1. Adhere the set of game cards for Activity 16 to tagboard. Color, laminate, and cut apart.
2. Draw smiley faces on an envelope for decoration and label (Fig. 1).
3. Put the game cards in the envelope.

Directions for Using

1. Two to four players can play this game.
2. Three cards are dealt to each player. The remaining cards are placed in a pile facedown. Turn the top card of this pile faceup and place it beside the pile.
3. Each player looks in his or her hand to determine if he or she has any sets of two pictures that begin with the same beginning sound. The player must say both words before laying the matching pictures down. If the player has a "Smiley Face" card, the player may pretend it is any word and make a pair. However, before the player can make a match with the "Smiley Face," he or she must say a word that begins with the same beginning sound as the word on the card with which the "Smiley Face" is being matched.
4. After all possible matches have been made, the player on the right of the dealer may choose to pick up the card that was turned faceup or the top card on the facedown pile. If that card provides a match for the player, the player must say both words and put the pair in front of him or her. If the card chosen by the player does not match, the player must put the card in his or her hand. One card from the player's hand must then be discarded by placing it faceup by the pile of cards.
5. The game continues until one player does not have any cards left. That player is the winner.

ACTIVITY 17

Auditory Skills—Level 3 (Memory)

Remember Me Tree

Directions for Making

1. Trace or duplicate the tree for Activity 17 so you have three trees.
2. Cut out and color the trees. Adhere one tree to the front of a folder for decoration and label (Fig. 1).
3. Adhere the other two trees inside the folder (Fig. 2).
4. Adhere the leaf word cards for Activity 17 to tagboard, laminate, and cut out. Place in an envelope on the back of the folder (Fig. 3).
5. Laminate the folder.

Fig. 1

Fig. 2

Fig. 3

Directions for Using

1. Two players can play this game with supervision.
2. Each player chooses a tree inside the folder.
3. Leaf word cards are placed facedown in a pile.
4. The leader or teacher draws a card and says the four words printed on the card.
5. The first player is asked to repeat the four words in order. If the player can repeat the four words in order, the player may take the leaf word card and place it on the tree.
6. The teacher reads a card to each player in turn, and the first player to fill a tree with leaves is the winner.

ACTIVITY 18

Auditory Skills—Level 3

Blasting Off

Directions for Making

1. Cut out and color the spacecraft for Activity 18, adhere it to the front of a folder for decoration, and label (Fig. 1).
2. Cut out and color the game board for Activity 18, join path, and adhere to the inside of the folder (Fig. 2).

43

3. Trace or duplicate picture cards for Activity 18 so that you have two sets.

4. Color the sets of picture cards. Adhere the sets to tagboard, laminate, and cut apart. Place in an envelope on the back of the folder (Fig. 3).

5. Laminate the folder.

Fig. 1

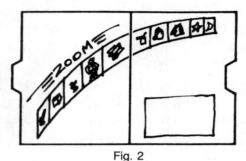
Fig. 2

Fig. 3

Directions for Using

1. Two players can play this game with supervision.

2. Each player is given a token. Both tokens are placed in "Blast Off" space to begin.

3. Place the eighteen picture cards facedown in rows—three across and six down.

4. Players in turn select a picture card and turn it over, trying to find a picture that will rhyme with the first picture (block) on the game board path. If the card does not match, the player must turn it back over and replace it in the same position. If a match is made, the player moves his or her token to the matched picture and the picture card is removed.

5. The matches must be made in order according to the next picture on path and each player must match every picture on the board. Remembering where each picture is placed as the cards are turned over and not used will give players an advantage.

6. The first player to find a rhyming picture for each picture on the game board path is the winner. That player has arrived at the moon!

ACTIVITY 19

Auditory Skills—Level 3 (Discrimination)

Jawsy-Clawsy

Fig. 1

Directions for Making

1. Adhere the pages for Activity 19 to tagboard. Color, laminate, and cut out.

2. Trace around two of the cards to make shark shapes for decoration on an envelope (Fig. 1). Label the envelope.

3. Put the word cards in the envelope.

Directions for Using

1. Two to four players can play this game.
2. Deal out all the cards.
3. All the players look to see if they have any pairs of cards with pictures that rhyme. If so, they lay the pairs down in front of them.
4. The first player then draws a card from the player on the left. If the new card forms a rhyme pair with a card in the player's hand, the new pair is laid down with the player's other pairs.
5. Game continues in this manner until one player is left with "Jawsy-Clawsy" card. This player is the loser and the player with the most pairs is the winner. Variation: These cards can also be used to play a game like Concentration, leaving the "Jawsy-Clawsy" card out.

ACTIVITY 20

Auditory Skills—Level 3 (Discrimination)

Pict-O

Fig. 1

Directions for Making

1. Cut out the four game boards for Activity 20. Duplicate any one of the game boards, color it, and adhere the copy to the front of a large envelope for decoration, and label (Fig. 1).
2. Color the four game boards, adhere to tagboard, and laminate.
3. Put game boards in the envelope.
4. Adhere the set of picture cards for Activity 20 to tagboard, laminate, and cut apart.
5. Put picture cards into a small envelope. Place the small envelope in the envelope with game boards.

Directions for Using

1. Four players can play the game, with another child as leader.
2. Give each player a "Pict-O" game board and several tokens.
3. The picture cards are placed facedown in a pile.
4. The child acting as leader chooses a picture card and says the name of the picture.
5. Each player looks on his or her game board for a picture that will rhyme with the word said. If the game board contains a picture that rhymes, the player covers it with a token.
6. The first player to fill a row vertically or horizontally, and name the rhyming words in that row, is declared the winner.

ACTIVITY 21

Auditory Skills—Level 3 (Discrimination)

Time Rhyme

Fig. 1

Directions for Making

1. Trace or duplicate the pictures of a tree and a bee on the game cards for Activity 21. Cut out and color. Adhere to the front of an envelope for decoration and label (Fig. 1).

2. Cut out and color Set 1 of the game cards for Activity 21. Put a green dot in the left-hand corner of each picture to identify this set of pictures. Adhere the set to tagboard, laminate, and cut apart. Put this set of game cards in one small envelope.

3. Cut out and color Set 2 of the game cards for Activity 21. Put a yellow dot in the left-hand corner of each picture to identify this set of pictures. Adhere the set to tagboard, laminate, and cut apart. Put this set of game cards in another small envelope.

4. Put both small envelopes into the larger labeled envelope.

Directions for Using

1. Two to four players can play this game with supervision.

2. Place all game cards faceup so all pictures can be seen.

3. Each player takes a turn matching a green game card with a yellow game card that rhymes. A minute minder is set and the player tries to make as many matches as possible within the one minute time limit. When the minute minder buzzes, it is the next player's turn.

4. The player with the most pairs when all cards are used is the winner.

ACTIVITY 22

Visual Skills—Level 1 (Discrimination and Memory)

Shape Up

Directions for Making

1. Cut out and color the two large geometric pattern cards for Activity 22, adhere to the front of the folder for decoration, and label (Fig. 1).

2. Color the geometric shapes on all the small pattern cards for Activity 22, using green, red, and yellow. Adhere the set of pattern cards to tagboard, laminate, and cut apart. Place in a pocket inside of the folder on the right side (Fig. 2).

3. Trace or duplicate the patterns of the square, circle, and triangle for Activity 22 so you have four of each. Color four red, four green, and four yellow. Cut out and adhere one of each of these shapes to the left side of the inside of folder (Fig. 2). Adhere the remainder

of the shapes to tagboard, laminate, and cut out. Place in an envelope on the back of the folder (Fig. 3).

4. Laminate the folder.

Fig. 1   Fig. 2   Fig. 3

Directions for Using

1. This is an individual activity requiring supervision.
2. Give the child a set of three different geometric shapes and a pattern card.
3. Tell the child to arrange the geometric shapes to reproduce the pattern shown on the card. For visual memory, tell the child to look at the pattern for approximately ten seconds. Then take the pattern card away and tell the child to reproduce the pattern without looking at the card.
4. Continue this part of the activity by using different pattern cards.
5. For the second part of the activity, give the child all the geometric shapes. Tell the child to sort the geometric shapes by putting them beside the matching shapes inside the folder.
6. The child can also sort the geometric shapes according to color.

ACTIVITY 23

Visual Skills—Level 1 (Discrimination)

Old MacDonald's Farm

Directions for Making

1. Duplicate five copies of the animal game board for Activity 23.
2. Color each animal the same color on all five copies.
3. Cut apart one game board of animals, adhere them to the front of a folder for decoration, and label (Fig. 1).
4. Adhere two complete game boards to the inside of the folder (Fig. 2).
5. Adhere the remaining two game boards to tagboard and color code by putting blue dots on the back of one and red dots on the back of the other. Laminate and cut apart to get two sets of animal cards. Place the animal cards in the envelope on the back of the folder (Fig. 3).
6. Laminate the folder.

Fig. 1

Fig. 2

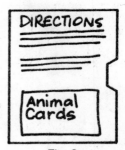

Fig. 3

Directions for Using

1. One or two players can play this game.
2. Each player chooses a game board on the inside of the folder and is given a set of animal cards.
3. Direct the children to turn one animal card over at a time, match it to the same animal on the folder, and cover entire game board as quickly as possible.
4. The first player to match all the animal cards to the board correctly is the winner.

ACTIVITY 24

Visual Skills—Level 1 (Discrimination)

Amos the Alligator

Directions for Making

1. Duplicate two copies of the Amos the Alligator card for Activity 24. Color and cut out the alligators, adhere to the front of an envelope for decoration and label (Fig. 1).
2. Adhere the set of playing cards for Activity 24 to tagboard. Color, laminate, and cut apart. Put playing cards into envelope.

Directions for Using

1. Two to four players can play this game.
2. Shuffle and deal out all the playing cards.
3. All the players look at their cards to see if there are any matching pairs. If there are, the players put the pairs down in front of them.
4. The first player then draws a card from the player on his or her left. If the new card forms a pair with a card in the player's hand, the new pair is placed with the player's other pairs.
5. Game continues in this manner until one person is left with Amos the Alligator. This player is the loser. The player with the most pairs of geometric shapes is the winner.

48

ACTIVITY 25

Visual Skills—Level 1 (Discrimination)

Face Me

Directions for Making

1. Trace or duplicate the four game boards for Activity 25 so you have two sets.
2. Adhere one set of game boards to tagboard, laminate, and cut apart. Put these gameboards in an envelope.
3. Use the other set of game boards to provide cover-up tokens for playing. Color code each set of these faces by making yellow dots on the back of the first set, green dots on the second set, red dots on the third set, and blue dots on the fourth set. Adhere to tagboard, laminate, and cut apart each square containing a face. Put each set of face tokens in a separate envelope.
4. Adhere the set of nine large face cards for Activity 25 to tagboard, laminate, and cut apart. Put face cards in another envelope.
5. Using a large envelope, draw a smiley face and a sad face on the front for decoration and label (Fig. 1). Place all the other envelopes with game parts in this large envelope.

Directions for Using

1. Two to four players can play this game.
2. Each player is given a game board and a set of face tokens.
3. The large face cards are turned facedown in a pile.
4. The first player turns a large face card over. Each player finds a face on his or her game board exactly like the one turned over.
5. Each player then finds a face token that matches that face and puts it over the face on the game board.
6. Play continues with the children revealing the large face cards in turn. The first player to cover a row of faces diagonally or horizontally shouts "Face Me."

ACTIVITY 26

Visual Skills—Level 2 (Discrimination)

Where Is My Mother?

Directions for Making

1. Cut out the largest duck for Activity 26, adhere to the front of the folder for decoration, and label (Fig. 1).
2. Using the medium-sized duck pattern for Activity 26, cut out ten white ducks. Write the following lower case letters on the ducks: o, h, u, a, r, m, n, c, b, and d. Adhere these ten ducks to the inside of the folder and draw a duck pond (Fig. 2).

3. Using the smallest duck pattern for Activity 26, trace or duplicate so you have sixteen yellow baby ducks. Cut out one baby duck and adhere to the front of the folder for decoration (Fig. 1). On the other fifteen yellow ducks, write one of the following lower case letters: o̲, h̲, u̲, a̲, r̲, m̲, n̲, c̲, b̲, d̲, t̲, p̲, s̲, e̲, g̲. Adhere the baby ducks to tagboard, laminate, and cut out. Place in an envelope on the back of the folder (Fig. 3).

4. Laminate the folder.

Fig. 1

Fig. 2

Fig. 3

Directions for Using

1. This is an individual activity.
2. Give the child the set of baby ducks.
3. Tell the child to look carefully at the letters on the mother ducks inside the folder and at the letters on the baby ducks.
4. Tell the child to match each baby duck with its mother who has the same letter and to put the baby ducks that do not match a mother duck in the duck pond.

ACTIVITY 27

Visual Skills—Level 2 (Discrimination and Memory)

Find Me

Fig. 1

Directions for Making

1. Following the bold lines, cut out the set of word cards for Activity 27. Adhere to tagboard, laminate, and cut apart. Put the word cards into an envelope.
2. Duplicate two sets of letters for Activity 27. Cut apart one set of letters and adhere to the front of an envelope for decoration, and label (Fig. 1).
3. Adhere the other set of letters to tagboard, laminate, and cut apart. Put these letter cards into the envelope.

Directions for Using

1. Two to four players can play this game.
2. Turn one word card faceup in front of each player.
3. Turn letter cards facedown in center of players.

4. Players take turns drawing letter cards. If the letter card drawn matches a letter in the word in front of the player, that letter is placed under the letter it matches. If the letter does not match, the player discards the letter back in the pile and reshuffles the letters.

5. The first player to match all the letters in the word is the winner.

ACTIVITY 28

Visual Skills—Level 2 (Discrimination)

Pinwheel Patty

Directions for Making

1. Cut out and color Pinwheel Patty for Activity 28, adhere to the front of a folder for decoration, and label (Fig. 1).

2. Trace or duplicate pinwheel for Activity 28 so you have four pinwheels. Cut out pinwheels and write the letters d, e, p, and k on one; f, u, b, and o on another; c, a, h, and n on another; and r, m, t, and s on the last one. Adhere the pinwheels to the inside of the folder and label (Fig. 2).

3. Adhere the set of letters for Activity 28 to tagboard, laminate and cut apart. Place letters in an envelope on the back of the folder (Fig. 3).

4. Laminate the folder.

Fig. 1

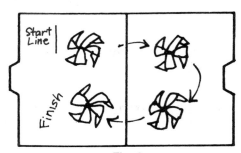
Fig. 2

Fig. 3

Directions for Using

1. Two to four players can play this game.

2. Give each player a token to place on start line.

3. Letter cards are placed facedown.

4. The first player draws a letter card. If the letter on that card appears in the first pinwheel, the player moves his or her token into the pinwheel. If the letter does not appear in the first pinwheel, the player stays on start line until the next turn. All letter cards are replaced in the pile and shuffled.

5. Each player draws a card in turn and, following the arrows, the players continue to move from pinwheel to pinwheel by matching the letter on the card drawn to the next pinwheel.

6. The first person to arrive in the last pinwheel is the winner.

51

ACTIVITY 29

Visual Skills—Level 3 (Discrimination)

Speed Along

Fig. 1

Directions for Making

1. Cut out racetrack for Activity 29 (including the center spinner board) and adhere to tagboard. Laminate.
2. Cut out flag for Activity 29. Adhere to the front of an envelope for decoration and label (Fig. 1).
3. Attach spinner in center of spinner board. Put racetrack in the envelope.

Directions for Using

1. Two players can play this game with supervision.
2. Each player is given a token to place at start line.
3. The first player spins the spinner and moves his or her token to the next space containing a word that contains the same <u>medial</u> letter as the one selected by the spinner.
4. Each player spins in turn and the first player to reach the word <u>win</u> is the winner.

ACTIVITY 30

Visual Skills—Level 3 (Discrimination)

Feed the Bunnies

Directions for Making

1. Trace or duplicate the large carrot for Activity 30 so you have two carrots. Color and cut out the carrots. Adhere carrots to the front of the folder for decoration and label (Fig. 1).
2. Trace or duplicate bunny and basket for Activity 30 so you have four bunnies and four baskets. Color and cut out baskets and bunnies. Adhere to the inside of folder and label baskets with the words <u>bar</u>, <u>men</u>, <u>tip</u>, and <u>dog</u> (Fig. 2).
3. Using the carrot pattern for Activity 30, trace or duplicate the pattern so that you have sixteen small carrots. Color the carrots and adhere to tagboard. Write the following words or nonsense words on the carrots: <u>beg</u>, <u>bap</u>, <u>bin</u>, <u>bor</u>, <u>mep</u>, <u>mag</u>, <u>mir</u>, <u>mon</u>, <u>ten</u>, <u>tar</u>, <u>tig</u>, <u>top</u>, <u>der</u>, <u>dan</u>, <u>dip</u>, and <u>dog</u>. Laminate carrots and cut out. Place carrots in an envelope on the back of the folder (Fig. 3).
4. Laminate the folder.

Fig. 1

Fig. 2

Fig. 3

Directions for Using

1. This is an individual activity.
2. Give the child the carrots with the "words."
3. Direct the child to open the folder and look carefully at the words on the baskets in front of the bunnies.
4. The child should begin by placing each of the carrots on the basket that has the word with the same beginning letter as that in the beginning of the word written on the carrot. After the child has done that, you can direct the child to place the carrots on the baskets according to the middle letter, and then the final letter.

ACTIVITY 31

Visual Skills—Level 3 (Discrimination)

Going Fishing

Directions for Making

1. Cut out and color the two large fish for Activity 31, adhere to the front of a folder for decoration, and label (Fig. 1).
2. Trace or duplicate the fish bowl for Activity 31 so you have two bowls. Label the fish inside one bowl with the following words: <u>on</u>, <u>dad</u>, <u>and</u>, <u>ton</u>, and <u>bat</u>. Label the fish inside the other bowl with <u>no</u>, <u>bad</u>, <u>end</u>, <u>not</u>, and <u>bet</u>. Adhere the fish bowls to the inside of the folder and draw a fish pond (Fig. 2).
3. Using the small fish pattern for Activity 31, trace or duplicate so you have fifteen fish. Label these fish with the following words: <u>on</u>, <u>dad</u>, <u>and</u>, <u>ton</u>, <u>bat</u>, <u>no</u>, <u>bad</u>, <u>end</u>, <u>not</u>, <u>bet</u>, <u>in</u>, <u>tin</u>, <u>pad</u>, <u>net</u>, and <u>but</u>. Adhere fish to tagboard, laminate, and cut out. Place the fish in an envelope on the back of the folder (Fig. 3).
4. Laminate the folder.

Directions for Using

1. Two players can play this game.
2. Each player chooses a fish bowl.
3. Place fish facedown in the fish pond.
4. The first player picks a fish from the fish pond. If the player can match the word on the fish to one of the words on the fish inside his

or her bowl, the player may keep the fish. If the fish does not make a match, the player replaces the fish in the fish pond and shuffles the fish.

4. The players pick up and match fish in turn, and the first player who matches all the fish in the fish bowl is the winner.

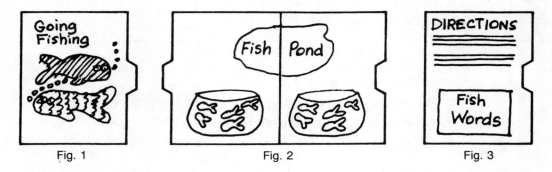

Fig. 1   Fig. 2   Fig. 3

ACTIVITY 32

Visual Skills—Level 3 (Discrimination)

Bumpy's Bone

Directions for Making

1. Cut out the bone for Activity 32, adhere to the front of an envelope for decoration, and label (Fig. 1).
2. Cut out the maze for Activity 32 and adhere to tagboard. Color Bumpy and his bone. Laminate and put the maze into the envelope.

Directions for Using

1. This is an individual activity.
2. Give the child a grease pencil.
3. Tell the child Bumpy wants his bone and the child must help him get it.
4. Ask the child to look carefully at the words in the four paths to find the word that is different in each set. This is the path Bumpy must use to get to the bone.
5. The child uses the grease pencil to draw a path through the words that are different in each set.
6. The game is finished when the child reaches the bone. After doing so, the child must point to the different word in each set to make sure the path is right.

ACTIVITY 33 (Discrimination and Memory)

Visual Skills—Level 3

Picking Apples

Directions for Making

1. Duplicate three copies of the tree for Activity 33.
2. Color the three trees. Adhere one tree to the front of a folder for decoration and label (Fig. 1).
3. Adhere the other two trees to the inside of the folder (Fig. 2).
4. Adhere the set of apple cards for Activity 33 to tagboard, laminate, and cut out. Put the cards into an envelope on the back of the folder (Fig. 3).
5. Adhere the set of word cards for Activity 33 to tagboard, laminate, and cut apart. Put the cards into another envelope on the back of the folder (Fig. 3).
6. Laminate the folder.

Fig. 1

Fig. 2

Fig. 3

Directions for Using

1. Two players can play this game.
2. Each player is given a set of five apple cards to place facedown on a tree inside the folder. The player can look at the apples before placing them facedown.
3. The ten word cards are shuffled and placed facedown.
4. The first player turns a word card over. Both players look at the card for approximately ten seconds. The card is then turned facedown.
5. Both players immediately begin turning their apples over to try and find the apple that has the same nonsense word as the one they just saw.
6. When a player finds the nonsense word on an apple, it is compared with the card that was turned up. If the card and the apple are exactly the same, the player keeps the apple. If they do not match, the apple is placed back on the tree.
7. Players turn over word cards in turn and the first player to pick all his or her apples from the tree is the winner.

55

FOUR FOUR FOUR FOUR FOUR

ADDITIONAL IDEAS AND MATERIALS FOR PARENTS AND TEACHERS

VISUAL-MOTOR COORDINATION

Level 1: Makes Gross Body Movements such as Required in Running, Hopping, and Scribbling

Additional Ideas for Home or School

1. **Balancing**

   Make a balance beam for children to walk across by simply putting a 2″ × 6″ board on two wooden or concrete blocks about eight inches off the ground. Ask each child to walk across forwards, sideways, and backwards. Observe if the child is able to balance.

2. **Mother, May I?**

   Play games like "Mother, May I?" in which you direct the children to do a variety of things involving motor coordination. This game is played by having a leader who gives each of the children in turn a command such as, "Take three hops on both feet," or "Take four giant steps." The children must remember to say, "Mother, may I?" before following the directions or they go back to the start line. The first child to get to the finish line is the winner.

3. **Drawing**

   Give children very large pieces of paper or old newspapers and crayons. Allow them to color or draw whatever they wish. Also, make available chalk, chalkboards, and easels for the children to draw and paint.

4. **Beanbag Throw**

   Using a large sheet of cardboard or wood, make a large hole or holes into which a beanbag can be thrown. A large clown head with a big mouth and the two eyes as openings makes an interesting beanbag throw. Prop the board against a wall and indicate where the children should stand. Show the children how to throw the beanbag through the holes, then give each child a turn. For variation, the holes may be of varying sizes and points awarded for the different holes. Scores can then be kept.

5. **Let's Dance**

   Many children enjoy dancing and moving to music. Play different types of music and allow the children to "do their own thing" as the music plays. Many commercial records, such as those by Ella Jenkins or Hap Palmer, are available in local record shops. Many of these records contain lyrics and tunes that suggest specific movements for young children. For example, songs such as "Colors," "Marching Around the Alphabet," and "Put Your Hands Up in the Air" direct the child to stand up, jump up, sit down, and so forth according to certain letters, colors, or sounds.

6. **Jump! Jump!**

   Have two children hold a rope still while another child jumps over it. The rope can be raised and lowered according to the ability of the child jumping. The rope also can be moved back and forth slowly when at a low height.

7. Watch the Ribbon

Following objects by moving the eyes, not the head, is a good visual exercise. This can be done by tying a ribbon on a hula hoop, and twirling the hula hoop around your body or arm as the children follow the ribbon with their eyes. Asking the children to follow the chalk as you make designs on a chalkboard is also fun. Simply holding a pencil in your hand and moving it from left to right or up and down can provide eye-movement exercise. Notice if each child's eyes move together.

8. Follow Me

Play a game with a child in which you do a movement and the child imitates you. For example, you can hop three times on one foot and then wait for the child to do it. Next, skip around the table and then ask the child to do that. You also can reverse the game and allow the child to make the movement and you do the imitation.

9. Pantomime

Ask a child to look through magazines and picture books to find pictures of animals or other moving objects. For each picture tell the child to act out the movements of the animal or object to see if you can guess what it is.

Commercial Materials for Home or School
A source list, by letter code, of the companies that supply these materials appears on p. 73.

1. Harmon Walking Rail (SE)

This walking rail slopes outward and downward from the center to each side. It is 8′ long, 7½″ high at the center, and 10″ wide.

2. Mess 'N Play Tray (CP)

This is a 23″ × 23″ tray which keeps the mess of finger painting and clay work inside a self-contained environment, making cleanup easier. It is made of washable, sturdy plastic.

3. Body Movement Floor Game (MB)

This colorful 22¾″ × 22¾″ floor game is designed to develop gross motor skills. The players retrieve tokens for placement on the game board by performing basic gross-motor tasks such as walking, jumping, rabbit hopping, duck walking, and puppy running.

4. Swingles (MB)

This activity includes two four-inch, soft-foam balls attached to separate handles and is designed for safe use and handling. Training the children's eyes to follow the motion of an object is made easy with this highly motivating, manipulative device.

5. Hippety Hopscotch (CEC)

This activity includes a roll-up, 31″ × 77″ plastic mat for use indoors or out, instructions, and plastic playing discs.

Level 2: Connects Dots; Reproduces Simple Geometric Shapes; Turns Pages of Books Carefully

Additional Ideas for Home or School

1. **Lacing**

   Lacing cards can be made from pictures that a child has colored in a coloring book. Adhere each picture to a piece of cardboard and punch holes about one inch apart around the outline of the picture. The child uses a shoelace, with a knot tied in one end, to lace in and out of the holes until the picture is outlined.

2. **Hanger Ball**

   Make a racket by forming a clothes hanger into a diamond shape and stretching material cut from panty hose over the hanger. Provide a small rubber-sponge ball or an aluminum foil ball. A child can use the hanger racket to bounce the ball up and down, or to bat the ball and try to make a basket in a wastebasket or bucket.

3. **Sand Play**

   Provide sand and allow the children to pour sand from one container to another. The children can use funnels, large- and small-necked bottles, plastic jars with lids, or other containers.

4. **Macaroni Necklace**

   Using various shapes and sizes of macaroni, allow the children to string these to make necklaces and bracelets. The macaroni can be painted with various tempera paints if color is desired.

5. **Ring Toss**

   Make a ring toss game using a Tinker Toy or dowel rod placed in the ground or in a block of wood, and rubber jar rings or rings cut from the plastic lids of coffee cans. Ask each child to try and ring the wooden stick. Scores can be kept if desired.

6. **Clothespin/Milk Bottle Drop**

   Use a wide-mouth quart jar and several clothespins for this game. Ask each child to try to drop the clothespins into the jar. Scores can be kept if desired.

7. **Trace Hands**

   Give the children large pieces of paper and crayons. Ask the children to place their left hands on the paper and trace around the hand. (Left-handed children trace right hands.) The children can draw around their hands several times to make designs or a collage of hands. The hands can be colored in various colors to make an attractive picture.

8. **Place Mats**

   Using plain pieces of paper of place-mat size or plain place mats, write the name of each member of a child's family on a place mat by making dots for the child to connect. Ask the child to follow the dots to form the letters. Then the child can make illustrations on the mat and color them. Cover with clear Con-Tact paper.

9. Pegboard Fun

This activity requires a pegboard, simple designs, pegs, and rubber bands. Show a child one of the designs and ask the child to put the pegs in the board to match the design. Then stretch a rubber band around the pegs.

10. Follow the Dots

Make or purchase dot-to-dot pictures for the children to complete. Encourage them to color the finished pictures.

Commercial Materials for Home or School

1. Stencils for Tracing (SE)

A set consists of thirty-six durable 6″ × 6″ cards divided into four general areas: geometric shapes, transportation, seasons, and animals. Both the stencils and cut-out designs are provided for greater utilization.

2. Sewing Cards (SE)

A set consists of thirty-two sewing cards with sixteen different designs, four needles, and eight colors of yarn. Fine-motor skills are developed by sewing directly on the cards.

3. Large Colored Beads and Patterns (SE)

A set contains 144 one-inch beads in six colors, two thirty-six-inch laces for stringing and sixteen plastic-laminated pattern cards.

4. Lacing Cards: Shapes and Numerals or Alphabet (TRC)

The shapes and numerals set includes sixteen lacing cards with basic geometric shapes and the numerals zero through nine. The alphabet set includes twenty-six lacing upper-case-letter cards. Each set has six colored laces. On each card arrows indicate the starting hole and direction of the first stitch.

5. Latch Frames (ETA)

This set of three carefully designed, heavy-duty wooden frames allows a child to gain manipulative skill while learning how to open and close common latches.

Level 3: Copies Most Letters; Cuts on a Straight Line; Generally Stays within the Lines when Coloring

Additional Ideas for Home or School

1. Coloring

Give the children coloring books and various pictures to color. Encourage them to try to stay within the lines. The children can cut out these pictures to give or mail to friends and relatives.

2. Newspaper Cutting

Give the children newspapers and ask them to cut out certain ads, pictures, or columns. Indicate the particular lines where they are expected to cut. This will give them practice in following straight lines.

3. Copy Me

Make various letters on a chalkboard or large sheets of paper and ask the children to reproduce the letters. Make dotted lines for a child to connect if the child has difficulty forming particular letters.

4. Body Letters

Ask a few children to lie down on the floor and make letters with their bodies. Several letters can easily be made by using one or two children, i.e., t, r, c, d, h, i, j, l, n, o, p, q, s, u, v, x, y.

5. Trace My Body

Provide large sheets of paper. Have one child lie down on the paper with arms and legs apart. Ask another child to trace around the child lying on the paper. Each child can then cut out his or her own body. Drawing the eyes, mouth, hair, or clothes on the body can also be fun. Then ask the children to color the forms appropriately to match what they are wearing that day.

6. Templates

Templates for the children to trace around can be made by cutting shapes or letters from cardboard or the plastic lids of coffee cans. Use a razor blade or sharp knife to cut out the shapes or letters. Both the forms and the letters can be used for tracing.

7. Chalk Fun

Most children enjoy working with chalk and the chalkboard. Provide each child with a small chalkboard and several pieces of colored and white chalk. Ask the children to draw circles, make letters, draw lines, and connect dots.

8. Guess My Letter

Make dot-to-dot letters for the children to complete. Provide directional arrows for letters such as k or N. Before a child follows the dots ask the child to guess what the letter will be.

Commercial Materials for Home or School

1. Sequential Development Alphabet Cards (SE)

A set contains forty plastic-laminated cards, 8½" by 11". Children can trace and reproduce letters. Each letter of the alphabet is given with directional arrows and beginning and ending dots.

2. Weaving Mats (SE)

A set contains twelve carefully designed, plastic-impregnated-material weaving mats, each 6¾" × 6¾", and 108 brightly colored slats in six assorted colors.

3. Alphabet Stencils (TRC)

A set includes plastic stencils for each letter of the alphabet. Stencil letters are ⅝" to 1⅛" high. An accompanying set of cards shows each letter with arrows showing the directions of strokes.

4. Visual-Motor Skills—Level A (CPI)

This is a set of liquid duplicators for tasks ranging in difficulty from easy stages of drawing within limits and tracing to the more demanding stages that involve completing and reproducing designs and patterned sequences.

5. Happy Happy Chalkboards (ISS)

These lap chalkboards, 17" × 26", are contoured to fit the body. The washable chalkboard finish is adhered to hardboard.

AUDITORY SKILLS

Level 1: Distinguishes and Remembers Grossly Different Environmental Sounds and Simple Rhythm Patterns

Additional Ideas for Home or School

1. **Tick-Tick**

   Hide a child's musical clock or a loud ticking clock while the children are out of the room. Ask the children to come into the room and find it by listening for the ticking.

2. **Guess Who I Am!**

   Blindfold a child and have several people with familiar voices (mother, father, friend, brother, sister) say a few words. See if the child can identify the voices. You may want to make a cassette tape for this activity with the familiar voices and/or other environmental sounds, such as a bird singing or a dog barking. With a tape, blindfolds are not necessary.

3. **Tap-Tap**

   Blindfold a child. Make tapping noises in different areas of the room. See if the child can indicate where you were when you made the sounds.

4. **Records**

   Many commercial records and cassettes are available that have rhymes, finger plays, and songs that children can listen to and then follow along. Some records and cassettes have directions that the children can listen to and follow. It is fun for parents and children to visit a record shop.

5. **Noisemaker**

   Make a grab bag containing various items that make noises, i.e., a whistle, a bell, a musical triangle, and a horn. Have one child reach into the bag and pull out a noisemaker while the other children turn their backs. Then the child makes a noise and the others guess what the noise is. The child who guesses the noise gets the next turn. To simplify the activity you may want to familiarize the children with the various items in the bag.

6. **Indian Games**

   Use a coffee can with a plastic top for a drum. Using a pencil, tap out various patterns, i.e., tap-tap-tap; tap-pause-tap-tap. Then ask a child to reproduce this. Also, a child can tap out patterns for you and then listen to see if you repeat them correctly.

7. **Matching Sounds**

   Use eight small opaque containers (frozen-juice cans or film cans). Put items that match in pairs of containers. For example, put small rocks in two containers, sand in two containers, cotton balls in two containers, and paper clips in two containers. Ask a child to shake the containers and match the pairs of containers that sound the same. You may want to color code the containers to make them self-correcting.

8. **What's That Sound?**

   Collect a variety of objects that can make noise. Ask the children to close their eyes while you make a sound. After the sound has been made, ask the children to guess what the sound was made with. The following sounds could be used: tearing or crumpling paper, tapping spoons together, blowing on a bottle, blowing a whistle, or pencil tapping.

9. **Snap and Seek**

   Show a child an object that you are going to hide somewhere while the child goes in another room. When the child returns and starts looking for the object, snap your fingers loudly when the child gets close. When the child moves away from the object, snap softly. The child must listen carefully for the snapping clues in order to find the object.

10. **Bottle Blow**

    Provide the children with bottles that are filled to various levels. Show the children how to blow across the bottles to make sounds. Discuss the different pitches—high to low. Have a child place the bottles in the order of high to low.

Commercial Materials for Home or School

1. **Shake and Match Sounds (TRC)**

   A set contains eight pairs of cylinders. Each cylinder contains an item (or items) that produces sound when it is shaken. Children are to shake the cylinders to match the ones that produce identical sounds.

2. **Rhythm Band Set (DFG)**

   A selection of drums, tambourines, cymbals, triangles, bells, and blocks can be used to make a rhythm band.

3. **Pretend (CEC)**

   The lyrics on this Hap Palmer record create magical moments of listening and inspire children to pretend. As the children listen, they are encouraged to react and create independently.

4. **Figure-Ground Discrimination—Vol. 2 (L)**

   The primary purpose of this record is to train the children to distinguish environmental sounds and to delineate and respond to relevant sounds as opposed to background noises.

5. **Counting Games and Rhythms for Little Ones (L)**

   This Ella Jenkins record or cassette guides children through rhymes and simple rhythmic activities. Children can clap, skip, and count along with Ella.

6. **Sounds in My World (ISS)**

   This listening skills program helps children to develop an awareness of environmental sounds, the ability to discriminate between them, and auditory memory. The program consists of two cassette tapes, a twenty-eight-page duplicator-master workbook, and ten sets of story cards.

Level 2: Discriminates Likenesses and Differences in Sounds in Initial Positions of Words; Can Repeat Three Related Words in Sequence

Additional Ideas for Home or School

1. **Sing a Song!**

   Play recorded songs such as "Going on a Bear Hunt," "Bingo," and "Old MacDonald Had a Farm." The repetition of these lyrics helps children improve their auditory skills.

2. Picture Sounds

Collect many pictures from magazines, newspapers, or catalogs of things that begin with the same sounds. For example, collect groups of pictures of things that begin with /m/, /b/, /t/, and /p/. Ask the children to say the names of these pictures and then separate them into piles according to their beginning sounds.

3. My Name

Write each of the children's names on a large piece of paper. Then ask the children to look through magazines, newspapers and catalogs, to find pictures of things that sound like the sound at the beginning of their names. The children can cut out the pictures and paste them on the papers under their names. For example, Jenny might find pictures of jewelry, junk, a jar, a jacket, jelly, and juice.

4. Going Shopping

Give a child a magazine, catalog, or newspaper and tell the child to go shopping for three objects, such as coats, pans, and toys. Ask the child to look for pictures of these items, cut the pictures out, and put them in piles. After a short period of time suggest three additional objects.

5. Puzzles

Using unlined 5″ × 8″ cards, glue two pictures of objects that begin with the same sound, i.e. a bat and a boy or a man and a map, on each card. Cut the two pictures on each card apart at an unusual angle. Mix the pieces together and ask a child to find the pictures whose beginning sounds are the same and fit them together. This activity is self-correcting.

6. Remember and Name

Ask a child to close his or her eyes. Make a series of sounds, identifying each sound by a number, i.e., snap your fingers and say "one," clap and say "two," crinkle paper and say "three." After completing three or four sounds, ask the child to name the sounds in the order they were presented.

7. Listening Poem

Go for a walk and listen for sounds. Upon returning from walk, ask the children to help you write a poem about the sounds they heard. You may write the first line and suggest that one child make up the next line, another child the third line, etc. For example:

Trains go swishing by,
Birds singing in the trees,
Children talking to each other.

8. Movement Game

Give directions for the children to follow, such as:

Anyone wearing blue, clap your hands.
Anyone wearing tennis shoes, jump up and down.
Anyone wearing a shirt, stand up and turn around.

9. Alike or Not

Say two words having similar sounds at the beginning or ending, such as dad and bad. Ask the children if you are saying the same word twice or two different words. Proceed by saying some words that are alike and others that are different. For example, you might say <u>bed</u> and <u>bad</u>, <u>dog</u> and <u>dot</u>, <u>jump</u> and <u>jump</u>, <u>cat</u> and <u>car</u>, and <u>saw</u> and <u>saw</u>. Make sure the children are not watching your mouth for clues.

10. **Number Please!**

It is very important for children to learn their telephone numbers. Therefore, teaching the children their telephone numbers is a meaningful way to work on auditory memory. Teach each child the first three numbers first. When the child can repeat these, teach the next four numbers.

Commercial Materials for Home or School

1. **Listen and Jump (SE)**

Game activities involve discriminating differences in sounds, synthesizing sounds into words, transferring words into visual symbols, listening, remembering, and following directions. Two to four players can participate.

2. **Smart Set (SS)**

This set of twelve ready-to-assemble readiness games covers auditory recognition of initial and final consonants and rhyming words.

3. **Auditory Discrimination—Beginning Sounds (MPC)**

This is a set of duplicating masters for activities that give children practice in the recognition of initial consonant sounds.

4. **It's Fun to Listen (MPC)**

A set includes cassette, eight color transparencies, and sixteen duplicating masters for activities that give the children practice in following simple directions and responding to auditory clues.

5. **Magic Cards—Initial and Final Consonants (ETA)**

These 8½" × 11" cards fit into plastic envelopes on which children can write. A set includes forty exercises on twenty cards. Rows of pictures appear and children are to mark those with the same beginning or ending sound.

6. **Beginning Sounds (MB)**

This set of sixty-four 4½" × 5½", colorfully illustrated cards is designed to train children in picture matching for beginning sounds.

Level 3: Discriminates Rhyming Patterns; Can Remember a Sequence of Four Unrelated Words

Additional Ideas for Home or School

1. **Nursery Rhymes**

Read nursery rhymes to the children, then talk about the words that rhyme and have the children think of other words that might rhyme with those words. Read part of a poem and ask the children to supply the missing word. For example, you might say, "Hey Diddle Diddle, the cat and the _____ ." A child should say "fiddle," and think of additional rhyming words such as <u>middle</u>, or <u>riddle</u>.

2. Rhyme Time

Repeat the following sentences and have the children try to supply a rhyming word. If the children cannot provide a word, you provide the word that rhymes. Help the children realize rhyming words sound alike except for a different sound at the beginning.

The great big cat
Ran after a little _____ .
There was a mouse
In the _____ .
The wind was right
To fly my _____ .
I'd like to take a look
At my new picture _____ .

3. Picture Rhymes

Place pictures of a man, a cat, and a chair on separate sheets of paper. Tell the children what the pictures are and talk about words that rhyme. For example, if you have a picture of a cat suggest bat, fat, flat, hat, mat, rat, and sat. Then ask the children to look for pictures in readiness workbooks, magazines, catalogs, and newspapers that would rhyme with any of these three pictures. When the children find rhyming pictures, they can cut them out and paste them on the sheet with the picture that rhymes. Encourage the children to make their own sets of rhyming pictures as well.

4. Remembering

Ask a child to listen carefully as you say a series of letters, words, or numerals. For example, say lunch, (pause), plant, (pause), coat, (pause), picture. Then ask the child to repeat these in the same order. This is a fun activity for long car rides or during waiting periods.

5. Rhyming Bag

Place various rhyming miniature objects or models in a box, such as a sock and a block, a fork and a cork, a shell and a bell, or a car and a star. Ask a child to match the rhyming objects.

6. Draw a Saw

Say some simple words such as bat, car, log, pan, or fall. As you say each word, ask the children tell you some words that rhyme with the word you just said. Then the children can draw pictures of the objects that rhyme.

7. Follow the Leader

Simple two-, three-, and four-step directions can be used to aid listening as well as memory. For example, tell a child to stand up, walk to the door, wave, and return to the chair. All the directions should be given before the child is allowed to carry them out.

8. Rhyming Art

Read a rhyme and then illustrate what you have said. For example, say "A funny clown ran around town. She had a green nose that looked like a hose." After each rhyme, draw a simple picture and discuss the words that rhyme. Ask the children to suggest other words that would rhyme with the rhyming words or perhaps make up a rhyme of their own.

9. Puzzle Rhymes

Cut pictures of objects that rhyme from magazines, coloring books, catalogs, or readiness workbooks. Adhere two pictures that rhyme to an unlined 5″ × 8″ card. Make at least four sets of these. Cut the pictures apart by using varied slants or curves. Give the sets of pictures to a child and ask the child to match the pictures that rhyme. This activity is self-correcting.

10. Riddle Rhymes

Young children love riddles! Make up riddles that include a statement about a word that rhymes. For example,

I am a dessert.
I can be made with cherries, apples, peaches, and many other fruit.
I rhyme with tie. What am I? (pie)

I have two legs.
I can talk.
I rhyme with can.
What am I? (man)

11. It's Me! I Don't Rhyme

Tell a child you are going to say four words. All the words will rhyme except one. Ask the child to listen carefully and then tell you which word does not rhyme. (You may need to repeat the words.) For example, you might say <u>ball</u>, <u>tall</u>, house, <u>call</u>. The child should tell you that house does not rhyme. This is an activity parents can use with a child as they are working around the house or driving on a vacation.

Commercial Materials for Home or School

1. Silly Sounding Rhymes—Set 1 (SE)

A set contains sixteen picture cards with rhyming verses. Each verse contains two rhyming words. The collection of rhyming words also provides introductory activities.

2. Rhyming—Level A (CPI)

This is a set of liquid duplicators for activities that introduce the rhyming concept and develop the initial stage of rhyming skills—discriminating between sounds that rhyme and those that sound grossly different.

3. Rhyming Pairs (ETA)

This set contains rhyme-matching picture cards that are divided into two parts by a curved cut, which makes the exercise self-correcting.

4. Listening Skills (ETA)

This kit consists of a record or cassette along with picture cards. After listening to the story, the child is asked to retell the story using the picture cards.

5. Rhythm and Rhyme (L)

This record allows children to explore their own sense of rhythm and innate appreciation of rhyme. The record includes hand rhythms and finger plays.

6. Objects That Rhyme (ISS)

This is a box of twenty toy models of everyday objects that rhyme.

VISUAL SKILLS

Level 1: Discriminates and Remembers Grossly Different Geometric Shapes

Additional Ideas for Home or School

1. **Puzzles**

   Many common items can be used for making puzzles. Cereal box fronts or backs are very colorful and interesting to young children. Also, inexpensive photographs of a child or family, or pictures the child has colored in a coloring book, can be adhered to cardboard and cut apart to make excellent puzzles. You should cut the pictures apart to correspond with the child's skill. Begin by cutting a picture into three pieces. If the child is able to put it together easily, cut the puzzle into four or more pieces. To keep the puzzle pieces separate, label each piece of a puzzle with a circle or some other shape.

2. **Sorting**

   Provide a child with different shapes of macaroni, coins, or other objects. Ask the child to separate the objects according to shape or size and place them in separate sections of an egg carton.

3. **Trace Me**

   Draw a circle, triangle, square, and rectangle on pieces of cardboard or plastic lids from coffee cans. Cut out the various shapes with a razor blade or sharp knife. Give a child the shapes as well as the outlines and have the child trace around the shape and the stencil from which it was cut. You can also use these as puzzles.

4. **Matching**

   Adhere various pieces of material, paint samples, or pieces of old wallpaper to squares of cardboard. Make two alike for each sample. Mix the samples together and then ask a child to sort them into matching pairs.

5. **Around the House**

   Show the children a geometric shape such as a circle, square, or triangle. Ask the children to look around the house or classroom to find other shapes like the one you are showing. For example, if you show a circle, the children may be able to point to a clock, lamp, or other circular objects.

6. **Find Me**

   On a large sheet of paper, trace around various items, such as a comb, cookie cutters, scissors, and fork. Give a child the items you traced and the large sheet on which you traced them. Ask the child to match the items by placing the objects on the tracings.

7. **Stickers**

   You can purchase many inexpensive stickers or seals that are appealing to children. There are usually seals with pictures of different animals or flowers, and for the different holidays. Adhere stickers to small business cards or unlined 3″ × 5″ cards, making two cards with each kind of sticker. Place the pairs of cards facedown. Tell a child to turn up two cards. If the two cards match, the child can keep them. If not, they are turned over in place. Begin by using three pairs of cards, and then increase to four or five pairs. You can also play "Old Maid" with these cards by taking away one sticker card so there is one that does not have a match.

8. Which One Is Missing?

Display a circle, a square, and a triangle. Tell a child to look at them carefully and then ask the child to close his or her eyes as you remove one of the objects. Then have the child look again and tell you which shape is missing.

Commercial Materials for Home or School

1. Sequential Sorting Box (SE)

This set consists of one hardwood cube, five wooden geometric shapes, and five interchangeable sliding panels for one side of the cube. Each panel has one to five geometric-shaped openings for the five red wooden shapes: circle, triangle, square, rectangle, and half circle.

2. Insert Puzzles (TRC)

A set includes a wooden puzzle board and sixteen insert pieces with large knobs for easy handling.

3. Sorting Card Set (TRC)

A set includes six decks of cards with pictures of animals, children, familiar objects, and geometric shapes and patterns. Each deck has a different background color and consists of twenty-seven cards (nine sets of three). Each deck can be sorted in several different ways.

4. Visual Discrimination—Level A (CPI)

This is a set of liquid duplicators for activities that provide practice in discriminating simple objects.

5. Free-Form Fit-Ins (ETA)

This consists of two sets of ten foam-rubber blobs that fit into two foam-rubber frames. Four different colors are available.

Level 2: Discriminates and Remembers Most of the Letters of the Alphabet

Additional Ideas for Home or School

1. Detective

Write an upper- or lower-case letter on a piece of paper. Give a child a catalog, magazine, newspaper, or cereal box. Ask the child to find and circle the letter that matches the one you have written on the paper.

2. Match-Up

Using unlined 3″ × 5″ cards, print one letter on both ends of each one. Cut the cards in half using various slants and curves. Mix the pieces and ask a child to put the cards together by finding the letters that look alike. If you are using letters such as b and p, make sure you underline the letters so the child will know the direction they should be turned. This activity is self-correcting.

3. Crazy Color

Take a picture from a coloring book and label the different parts of the picture with letters. For example, label each part with either y for yellow, b for blue, r for red, or o for orange. On the bottom of the page, write the corresponding letters using the appropriate crayon to indicate the color. (That is, write the letter in the same color as you want the child to color the labeled part.) Direct the child to color the picture by following the scheme. In doing so, the child will have to remember the colors associated with the different letters.

4. Oops!

Use a 3′ × 3′ piece of material cut from an old plastic tablecloth or sheet for this activity. Divide the sheet into nine sections and print a letter in each section. Also print these letters on nine separate unlined 3″ × 5″ cards. Place the cards facedown in a pile. The players take turns drawing four cards. Each player must put a foot or hand on each of the letters on the plastic sheet that match the letters on the cards. The winner is the player who successfully puts all four limbs on the correct letters without falling.

5. Old Maid

Make matching pairs of letters on unlined 3″ × 5″ cards. Also draw a picture of something the children do not like on one of the cards. For example, you might draw a picture of some food children don't usually like, or something else that has an unpleasant connotation. Shuffle the cards and deal them to each player. The players take turns drawing from one another in rotation. If the player gets two letters that match, the player places the pair in the center of the table. The player who has the undesirable picture at the end of the game is the loser; the player with the most pairs is the winner.

6. Try Me, I'll Fit

Using an old puzzle that is inlaid, put letters on the back of the puzzle pieces and the matching letters on the areas where each puzzle piece fits. The children can fit the puzzle together by matching the letters.

7. Take Away

Using magnetic letters, display a child's name. Tell the child to look carefully and then close his or her eyes. While the child's eyes are closed, remove one of the letters. Ask the child to look at the name again and tell you which letter is missing.

8. Letter Sort

Label several empty milk cartons or plastic containers with different letters. Give a child a set of cardboard or plastic letters and ask the child to sort the letters by putting them into the appropriate containers.

Commercial Materials for Home or School

1. Visual Discrimination—Level C (CPI)

This is a set of liquid duplicators for activities that provide practice in discriminating letter forms and word forms.

2. Sandpaper Letters or Numerals (ETA)

This set includes large sandpaper figures mounted on sturdy, tempered-masonite boards. As a child traces the rough sandpaper figures, the child feels the difference in the formation of the letters and numerals.

3. Picture Lotto (ETA)

This set consists of six boards and fifty-four picture cards with brightly colored children-oriented designs.

4. **Letter Recognition and Sorting Strip Books (ETA)**

   A set consists of eight books. Each page is cut into three strips with a letter on each strip. The child flips the strips until three letters are matched.

5. **Letter Discrimination Board (ETA)**

   A set consists of four boards. These boards introduce complete letter forms and provide simple exercises in discriminating and matching.

Level 3: Discriminates Words in Which the Letters are Different in the Initial, Medial, and Final Positions; Remembers a Sequence of Three Letters

Additional Ideas for Home or School

1. **Word Hunt**

   Write a common word such as the, and, if, she, he, or I on a piece of paper. Provide a child with a newspaper, magazine, or cereal box, and ask the child to find that word and circle it.

2. **Word-O**

   Write a simple word on an unlined 3″ × 5″ card. Give a child a set of alphabet letters (cardboard or plastic) and ask the child to find the letters to reproduce the word you have written. The child can put the letters under each of the letters in the word you have written.

3. **Find Me!**

   Use unlined 3″ × 5″ cards to make word cards for signs that are commonly seen in your neighborhood, such as the name of your street, stop, school, parking, exit, and names of stores. Give these to a child when you go driving, shopping, or walking, and suggest that the child try to find these words on signs. You can do this with letters on cards also, asking the child to find certain letters in words as you are driving or walking along.

4. **Cut and Paste**

   Write a child's name or other familiar name on an 8″ × 10″ sheet of paper. Give the child plenty of magazines, newspapers, or cereal boxes and ask the child to find words with letters to match the letters in the name you have written. The child can cut the letters out and glue them below what you have written or simply circle the letters that match.

5. **Hey, Look Me Over!**

   Use unlined 3″ × 5″ cards to make a set of word cards for the following words: cat, dog, cup, dig, she, we, dad, mom, are, eat, saw, out, for, can, see, has, was, run, new, his, her, the, you, boy, not, and but. Give a child the word cards and ask the child to put them in piles according to the first letter. When the child can do this successfully, ask the child to put them in piles according to the last letter of each word. Finally, ask the child to put the cards in piles according to the middle letter in each word. If you want to make this activity a game, you can time the child and see if he or she can beat a previous time.

6. Be Careful

Use unlined 3″ × 5″ cards to make two word cards for each one of the following words: <u>ba</u>d, <u>da</u>d, <u>wha</u>t, <u>whe</u>n, <u>ho</u>w, <u>no</u>w, <u>wen</u>t, <u>wan</u>t, <u>wa</u>s, <u>sa</u>w, <u>sa</u>y, <u>sta</u>y, <u>ma</u>de, <u>ma</u>ke, <u>si</u>t, <u>si</u>x, <u>sto</u>re, stove, <u>mu</u>st, <u>muc</u>h, <u>the</u>n, <u>tha</u>n, <u>wer</u>e, <u>whe</u>re, <u>ha</u>s, and <u>ha</u>d. Before playing any games with the children using these words, put the commonly confused pairs next to each other and have the children point out the differences. For example, display the word cards with <u>ba</u>d and <u>da</u>d. Have the children point out how the words are alike and different. After the children have seen the differences you can use these cards to play Concentration. The number of pairs that you use will depend upon the children's abilities. Place the word cards facedown. Have the children alternate turns turning over two cards. If the cards match, the player keeps the pair and gets another turn. If the cards do not match, the player replaces the cards in the same location. The player with the most pairs at the end of the game is the winner!

Commercial Materials for Home or School

1. Key Words Lotto 1 (ETA)

This activity includes four game boards with twenty words printed on each. Separate word cards are provided to match the words on the board.

2. Letter Recognition and Sorting Strip Books (ETA)

The pages of these books are cut into strips with letter combinations on each strip. The child flips the strips until three letter combinations are matched.

3. Primary Plastic Letters (ETA)

Each set consists of thirty-one letters which are 1½″ high. Using two sets, these letters can be placed in combinations for a child to match.

4. Sentence-Building Word Cards (ETA)

A set consists of one hundred laminated cards that a child can sort according to beginning letters that are the same.

5. Giant Picture and Word Matching Cards (ETA)

A set includes sixty-two 8″ × 11½″ plastic-laminated wall cards in full color with a title printed under each picture. Sixty-eight additional cards with words only are provided for matching.

NAMES AND ADDRESSES OF PUBLISHING COMPANIES

CEC   Childcraft Education Corp.
20 Kilmer Road
Edison, NJ 08817

CPI   Continental Press, Inc.
127 International Blvd.,
N.W.
Atlanta, GA 30303

CP   Constructive Playthings
11100 Harry Hines Blvd.
Dallas, TX 75229

DFG   Designs for Growing
P.O. Box 12085
Fort Worth, TX 76116

ETA   Educational Teaching Aids
159 West Kenzie Street
Chicago, IL 60610

ISS   Ideal School Supply Co.
11000 S. Lavergne Ave.
Oak Lawn, IL 60453

L   Lyons
530 Riverview Ave.
Elkhart, IN 46514

MB   Milton Bradley Educational
Materials
Springfield, MA 01101

MPC   Milliken Publishing Co.
1100 Research Blvd.
St. Louis, MO 63132

SS   Shakean Stations
P.O. Box 68
Farley, IA 52046

SE   Special Education and
Early Learning Catalog
Cole Supply
P.O. Box 1717
Pasadena, TX 77501

TRC   Teaching Resources Corp.
100 Boyleston Street
Boston, MA 02116

APPENDIX
APPENDIX
APPENDIX
APPENDIX
APPENDIX

READY-TO-REPRODUCE
SKILLS TESTS AND ACTIVITIES

SKILLS TEST 1

Visual-Motor Coordination—Level 1

SKILLS TEST 2

Visual-Motor Coordination—Level 2

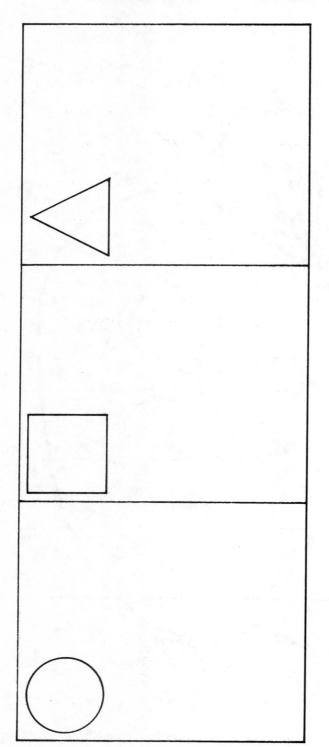

SKILLS TEST 3

Visual-Motor Coordination—Level Three (Upper-Case Letters)

A —— - - - - ——	B —— - - - - ——	C —— - - - - ——
D —— - - - - ——	E —— - - - - ——	F —— - - - - ——
G —— - - - - ——	H —— - - - - ——	I —— - - - - ——
J —— - - - - ——	K —— - - - - ——	L —— - - - - ——
M —— - - - - ——	N —— - - - - ——	O —— - - - - ——

SKILLS TEST 3 (continued)

P ___	Q ___	R ___
S ___	T ___	U ___
V ___	W ___	X ___
Y ___	Z ___	

SKILLS TEST 4

Visual-Motor Coordination—Level 3 (Lower-Case Letters)

a	b	c
d	e	f
g	h	i
j	k	l
m	n	o

SKILLS TEST 4 (continued)

p	q	r
s	t	u
v	w	x
y	z	

SKILLS TEST 5

Auditory Skills—Level 1 (Discrimination)

SKILLS TEST 6

Auditory Skills—Level 1 (Memory)

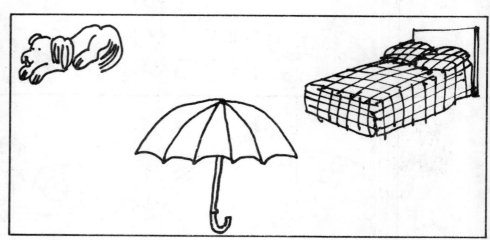

SKILLS TEST 7

Auditory Skills—Level 2 (Discrimination)

SKILLS TEST 7 (continued)

SKILLS TEST 8

Auditory Skills—Level 2 (Memory)

1.

2.

3.
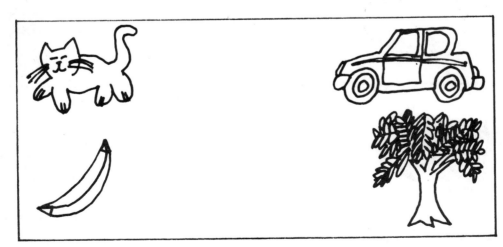

SKILLS TEST 9

Auditory Skills—Level 3 (Discrimination)

SKILLS TEST 9 (continued)

SKILLS TEST 10

Auditory Skills—Level 3 (Memory)

1.

2.

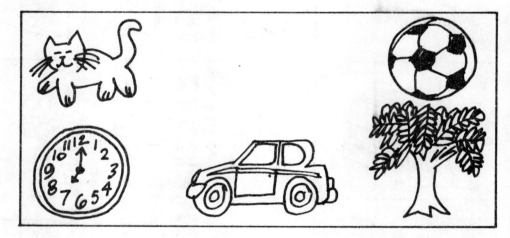

3.

SKILLS TEST 11

Visual Skills—Level 1 (Discrimination)

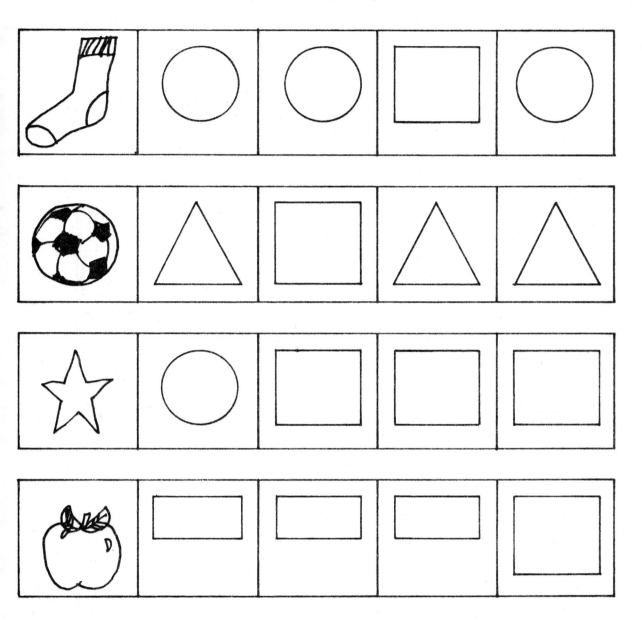

SKILLS TEST 12

Visual Skills—Level 1 (Memory)

SKILLS TEST 13

Visual Skills—Level 2 (Discrimination)

1	r	r	j	r
2	t	l	l	l
3	c	c	o	c
4	g	g	g	p
5	a	c	a	a
6	u	n	n	n
7	e	c	e	e
8	m	m	n	m
9	v	u	v	v
10	b	b	d	b
11	E	E	E	F
12	R	P	R	R

SKILLS TEST 14

Visual Skills—Level 2 (Memory)

1	S	T	A	C	B
2	T	A	C	B	S
3	A	C	B	S	T
4	C	B	S	T	A
5	B	S	T	A	C

SKILLS TEST 15

    Visual Skills—Level 3 (Discrimination)

1	fan	fan	gan	fan
2	bad	bad	bad	dad
3	hed	hed	ked	hed
4	nan	man	man	man
5	bit	bid	bid	bid
6	wod	wob	wod	wod
7	pac	pac	pac	pao
8	rim	rin	rin	rin
9	ten	tin	ten	ten
10	pod	pad	pod	pod
11	hum	hum	hum	hnm
12	gab	gob	gab	gab

SKILLS TEST 16

Visual Skills—Level 3 (Memory)

1	tba	bat	tab	bta
2	tba	bta	bat	tab
3	bta	bat	tab	tba
4	bat	tab	tba	bta

Visual-Motor Coordination—Level 1

Creepy Creatures

ACTIVITY 1 (continued)

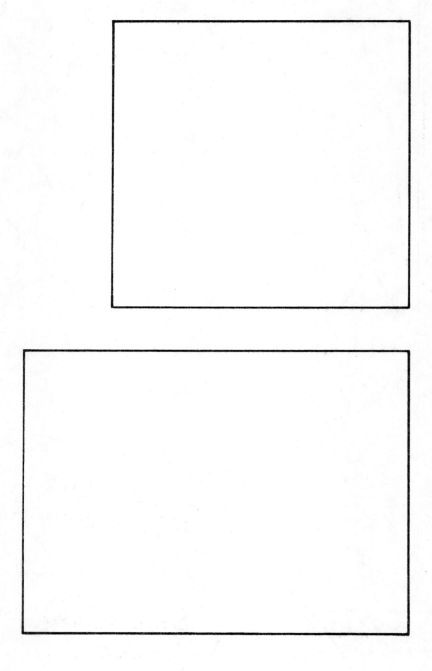

Visual-Motor Coordination—Level 1

Hippity Hop

**Large Foot and Footprint
Direction Cards**

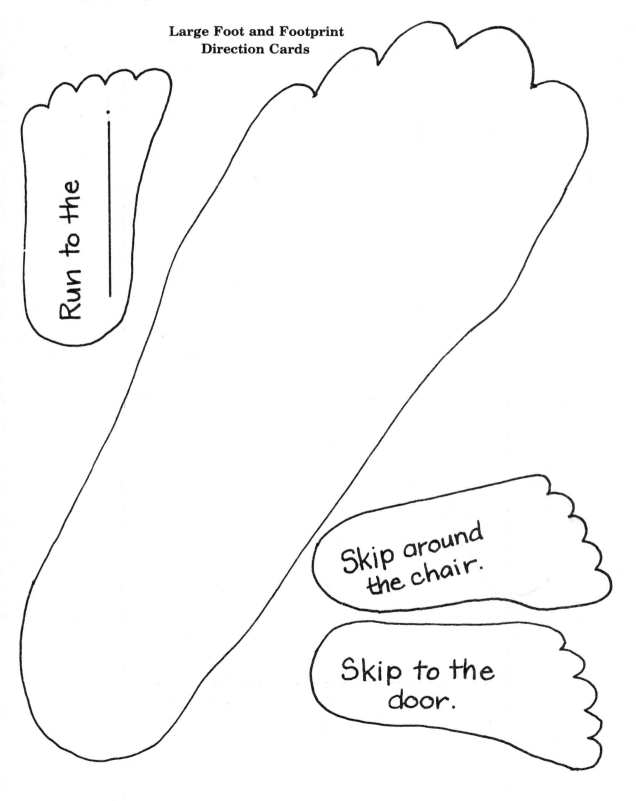

Run to the ___

Skip around the chair.

Skip to the door.

Footprint Direction Cards

Hop three times on the left foot.

Hop backwards two times on both feet.

Hop three times on the right foot.

Jump to the _____.

Hop forward four times on both feet.

Hop to the _____ _____.

Run to _____.

Hop on one foot to the _____.

Skip to _____.

Hop to the door.

Visual Motor Coordination—Level 1

Guess Who I Am!

Animal Playing Cards

dog	rabbit
horse	bird
snake	kangaroo
elephant	turtle

Visual-Motor Coordination—Level 2

Lace Me Up!

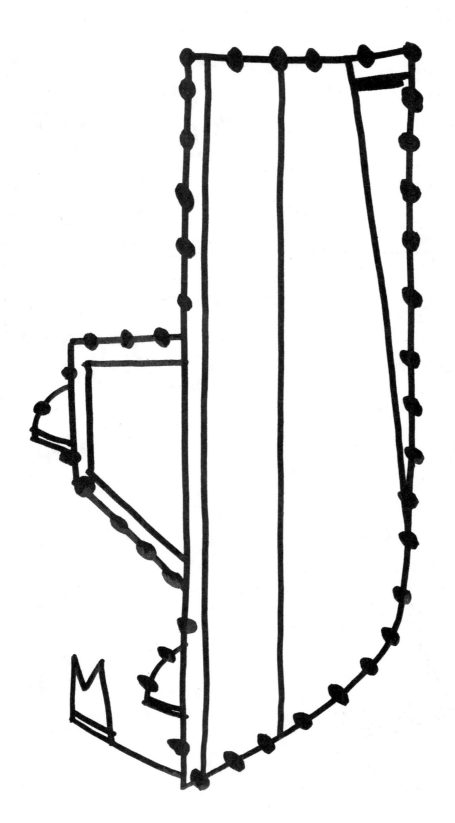

ACTIVITY 5

Visual-Motor Coordination—Level 2

Crazy Shapes

Cards

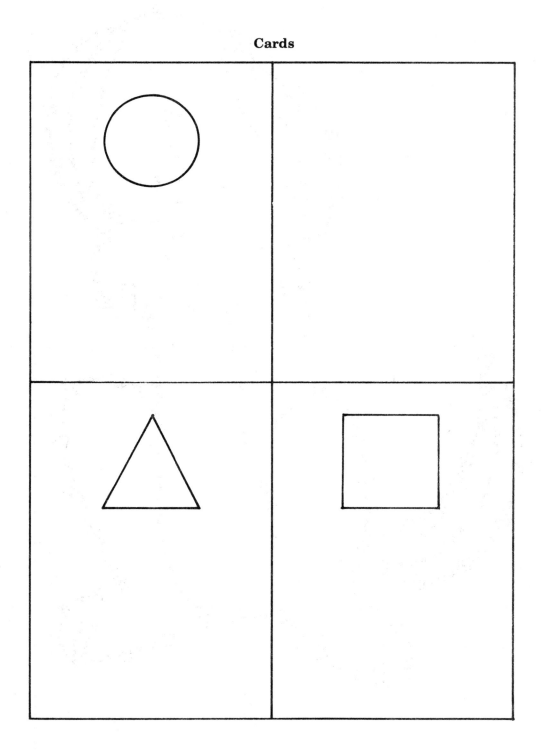

Visual-Motor Coordination—Level 2

Dashing with Dots to Monsterville

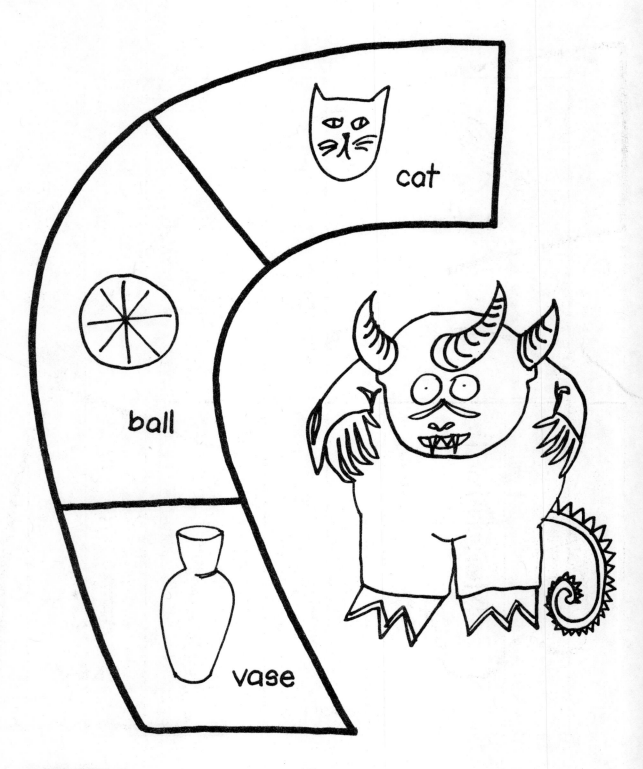

cat

ball

vase

Paths and Monsterville

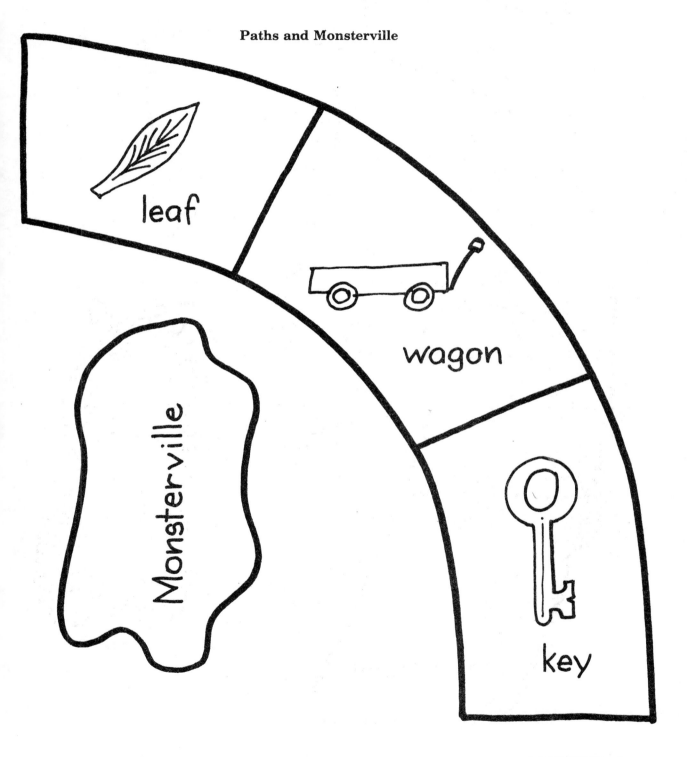

leaf

wagon

key

Monsterville

Dot Pictures

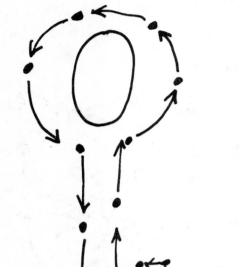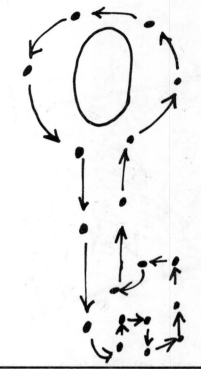

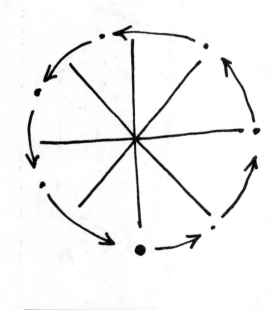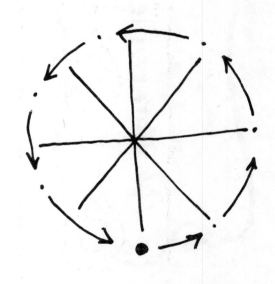

Dot Pictures

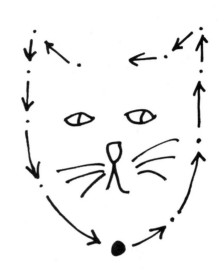

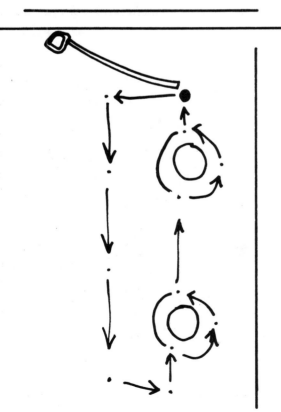

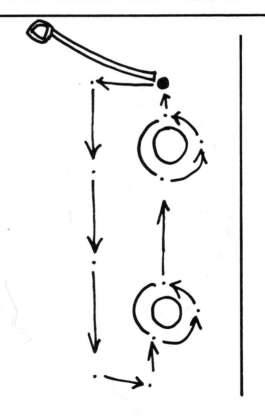

Dot Pictures

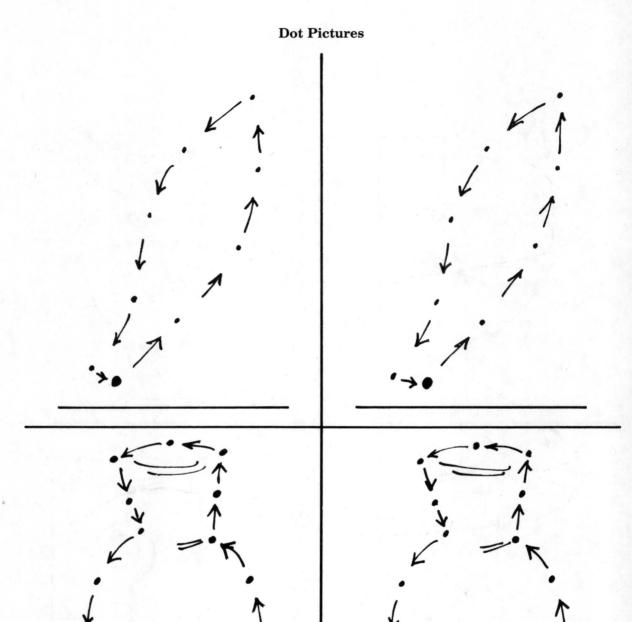

Visual-Motor Coordination—Level 2

Fishing For Shapes

109

ACTIVITY 8

Visual-Motor Coordination—Level 3

And We're Off!

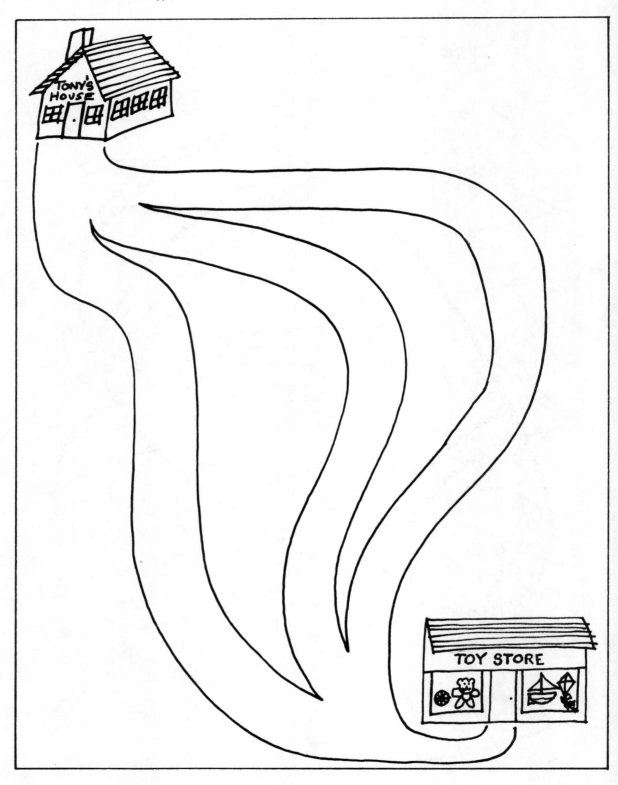

Visual-Motor Coordination—Level 3

Color Me

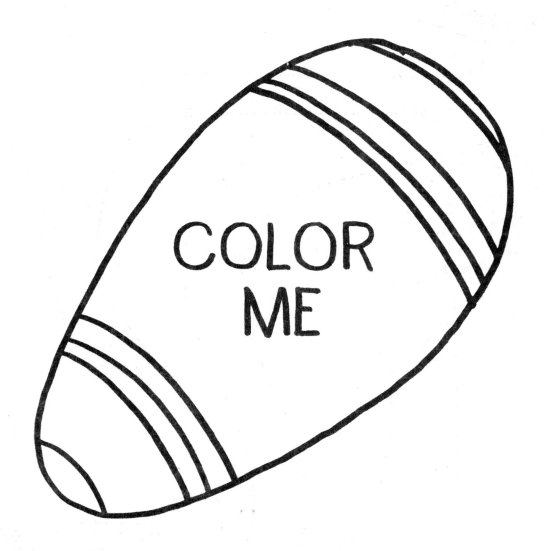

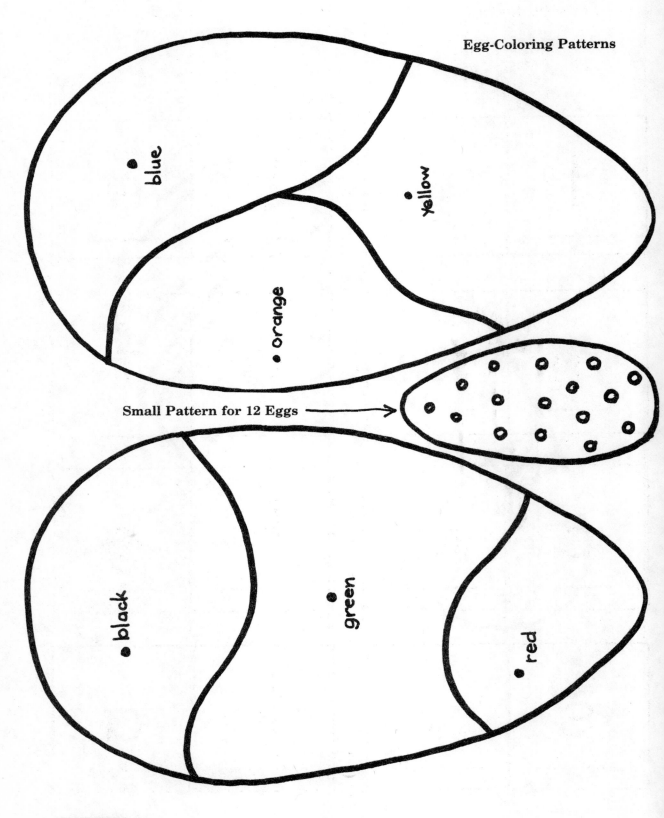

Egg-Coloring Patterns

blue

yellow

orange

Small Pattern for 12 Eggs ⟶

black

green

red

Visual-Motor Coordination—Level 3

Letter Dominoes

Domino Cards

t	c
b	**e**

m	s
g	**f**

a	m
h	**g**

s	y
k	**a**

Domino Cards

n	f		e	f
w	s		a	k
m	y		b	w
t	b		t	

Domino Cards

y	

n̲	

g	

w̲	

h	

n̲	

k	

h	

Auditory Skills—Level 1 (Memory)

Indian Signals

Indian and Smoke Signals

Indian Head and Feather Pattern

Clapping-Tapping Cards

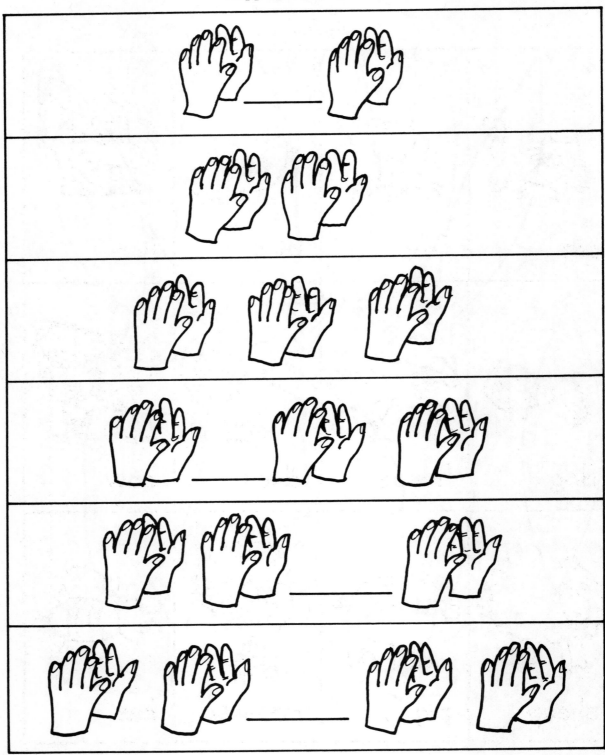

ACTIVITY 12

Auditory Skills—Level 1 (Discrimination)

Animal Sounds

Animal Cards

cat	frog	bird	lion
dog	horse	duck	cow
sheep	pig	rooster	bee

ACTIVITY 13

Auditory Skills—Level 2 (Discrimination)

Let's Build a Car

Car

Car Parts

Picture Cards

cat bat	man fan
gun gun	shoe shoe
cake rake	boat coat
tree tree	flag flag

Picture Cards

ACTIVITY 14

Auditory Skills—Level 2 (Discrimination)

Otto the Octopus

Plain Octopus

ACTIVITY 14

Decorated Octopus

Decorated Octopus

Picture Cards

cake	nurse
fan	man
soap	rake
dog	table

Picture Cards

gate

bed

lock

hat

steps

dress

man

cheese

Auditory Skills—Level 2 (Memory)

Pete the Repeat

Game Board

Game Board

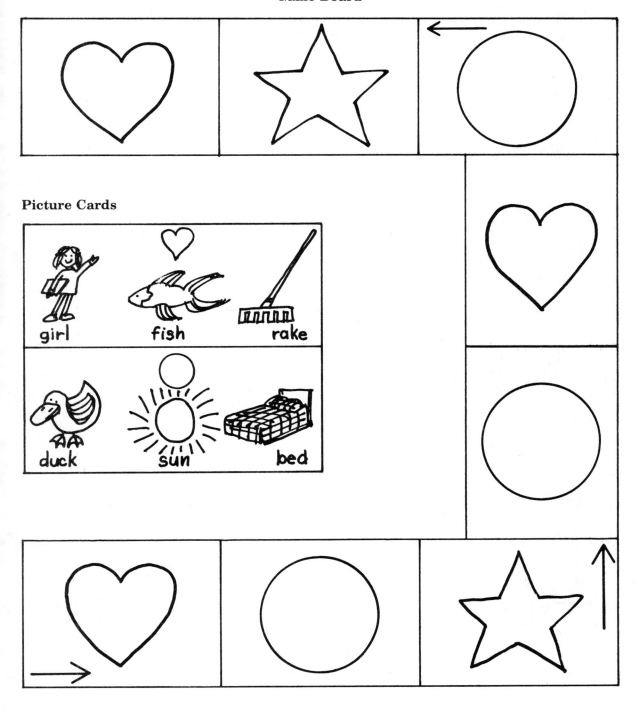

Picture Cards

girl   fish   rake

duck   sun   bed

Picture Cards

ACTIVITY 16

Auditory Skills—Level 2 (Discrimination)

Smiley Face

Game Cards

Game Cards

Auditory Skills—Level 3 (Memory)

Remember Me Tree

Tree

Leaf Word Cards

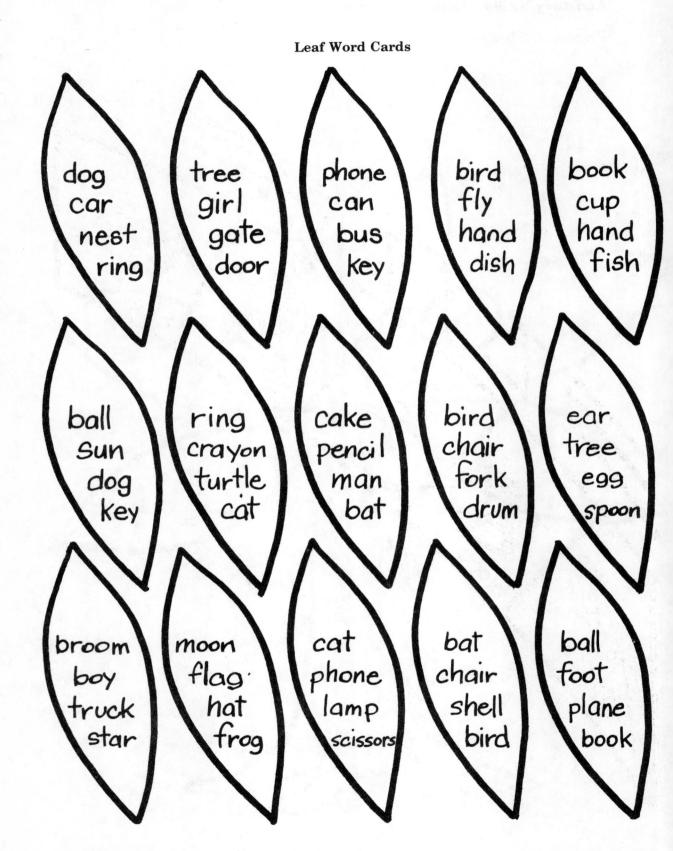

ACTIVITY 18

Auditory Skills—Level 3

Blasting Off

Game Board

ACTIVITY 18 (continued)

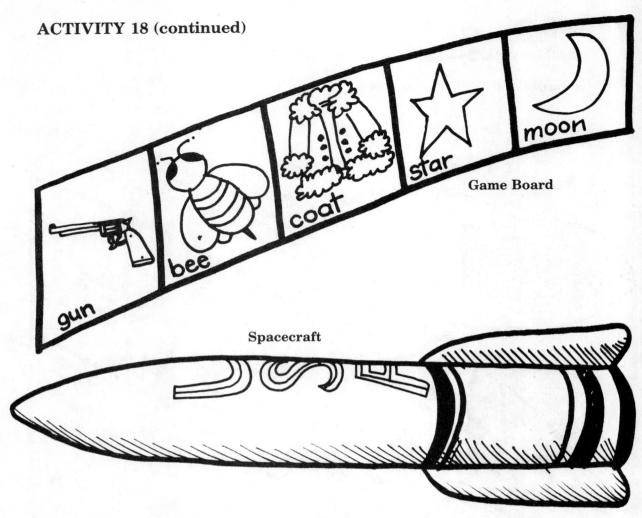

Game Board

Spacecraft

Picture Cards

ACTIVITY 19

Auditory Skills—Level 3 (Discrimination)

Jawsy-Clawsy

Word Cards

bed

sled

tree

bee

bat

cat

Jawsy-Clawsy Card

ACTIVITY 19

Word Cards

coat

boat

dog

frog

gun

sun

cake

rake

fan

can

Word Cards

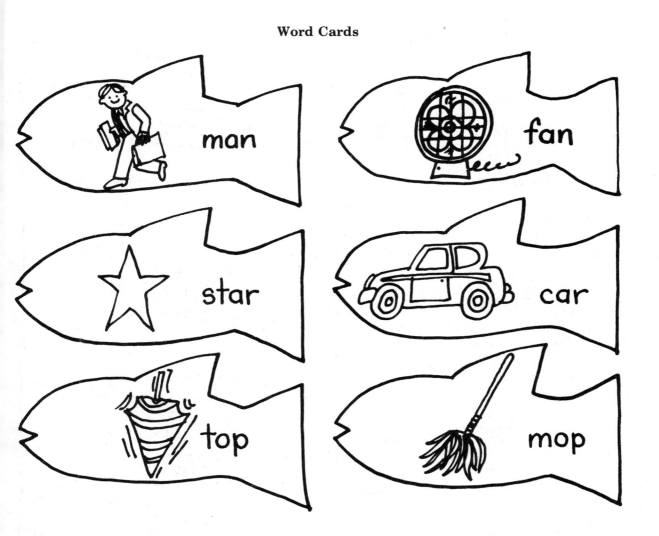

man

fan

star

car

top

mop

ACTIVITY 20

Auditory Skills—Level 3 (Discrimination)

Pict-O

Picture Cards

pie

hair

swing

gun

cat

duck

cone

bread

bug

Game Board 1

chair	ring	hat
eye	bone	sun
bed	rug	truck

Game Board 2

Game Board 3

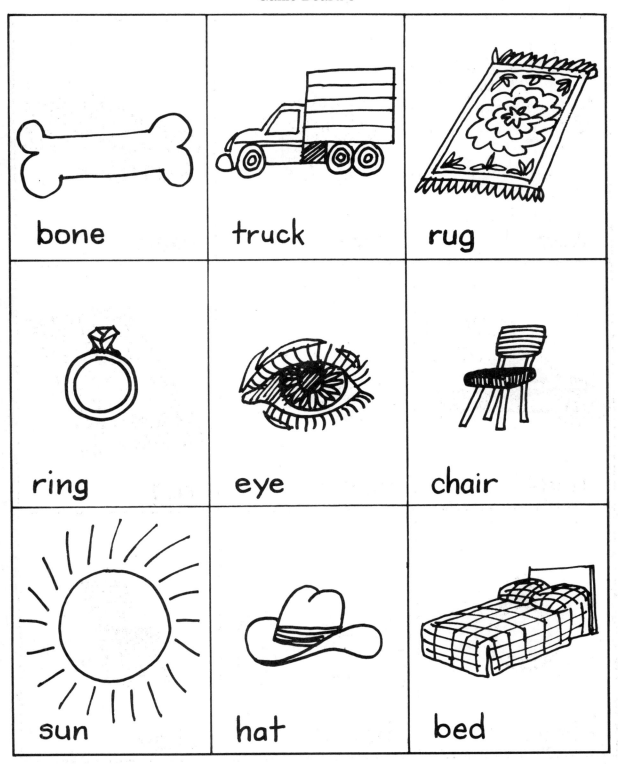

bone	truck	rug
ring	eye	chair
sun	hat	bed

Game Board 4

chair	ring	hat
eye	bone	sun
bed	rug	truck

ACTIVITY 21

Auditory Skills—Level 3 (Discrimination)

Time Rhyme

Game Cards, Set 1

swing	tree	top
hair	pan	car
cat	bed	trunk
boat	phone	yarn

Game Cards, Set 2

coat	bee	barn
mop	ring	bone
bat	skunk	star
sled	fan	stairs

ACTIVITY 22

Visual Skills—Level 1 (Discrimination and Memory)

Shape Up

Geometric Pattern Cards

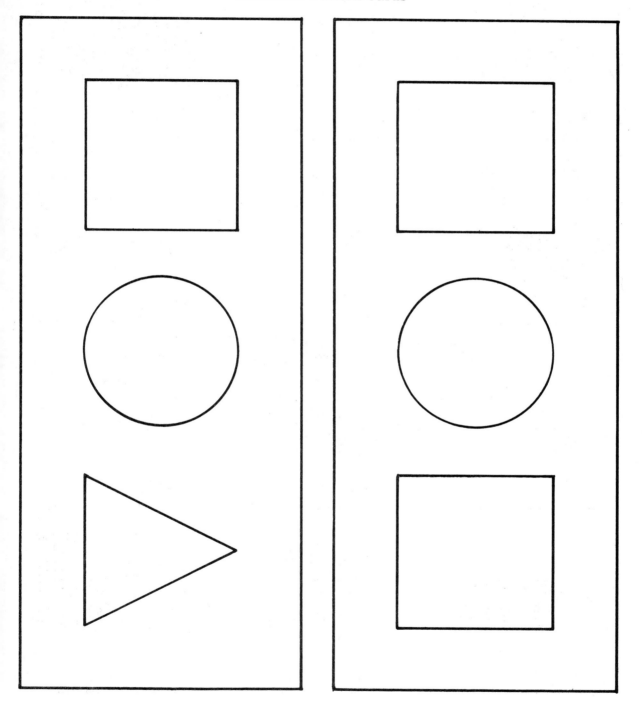

Pattern Cards

Geometric Shapes

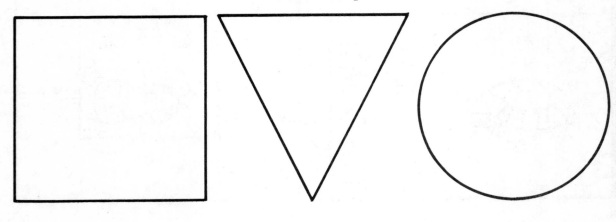

ACTIVITY 23

Visual Skills—Level 1 (Discrimination)

Old MacDonald's Farm

Animal Game Board

ACTIVITY 24

Visual Skills—Level 1 (Discrimination)

Amos the Alligator

Amos the Alligator

Playing Cards

Playing Cards

Visual Skills—Level 1 (Discrimination)

Face Me

Large Face Cards

Game Boards

Large Face Cards

Game Boards

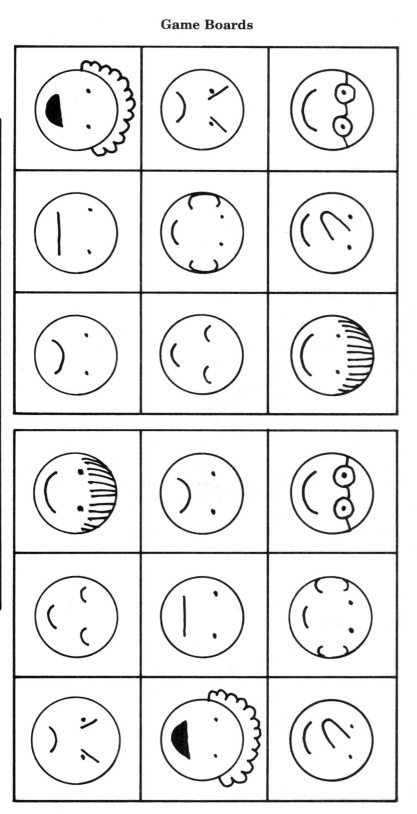

Visual Skills—Level 2 (Discrimination)

Where Is My Mother?

Ducks

ACTIVITY 27

Visual Skills—Level 2 (Discrimination and Memory)

Find Me

Word Cards

c	a	k	e

d	u	c	k

b	e	a	r

l	i	o	n

ACTIVITY 27

Letters

<u>a</u>	<u>a</u>	<u>a</u>	<u>a</u>
<u>e</u>	<u>e</u>	<u>e</u>	<u>e</u>
<u>i</u>	<u>i</u>	<u>i</u>	<u>o</u>
<u>o</u>	<u>o</u>	<u>u</u>	<u>u</u>
<u>u</u>	<u>c</u>	<u>c</u>	<u>c</u>
<u>k</u>	k	k	<u>d</u>
<u>d</u>	b	b	r
<u>l</u>	<u>n</u>	<u>l</u>	<u>n</u>

ACTIVITY 28

Visual Skills—Level 2 (Discrimination)

Pinwheel Patty

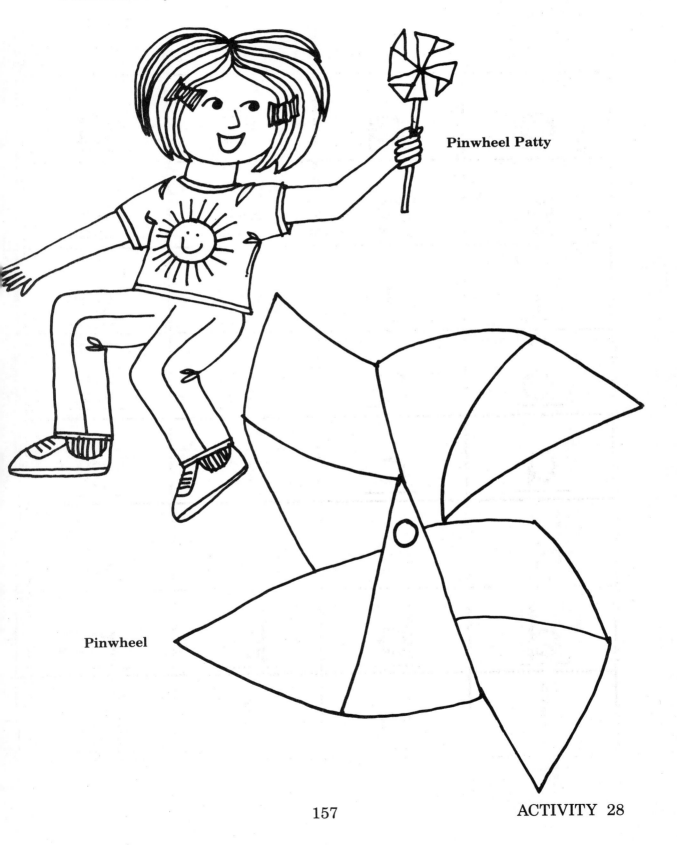

Pinwheel Patty

Pinwheel

ACTIVITY 28

Letters

t	m	s	o	a	c
f	h	p	n	m	r
h	k	u	e	b	d
e	b	j	l	n	o
u	n	z	t	m	s
a	c	f	g	p	q
x	r	h	k	v	y

Visual Skills—Level 3 (Discrimination)

Speed Along

Flag

Racetrack

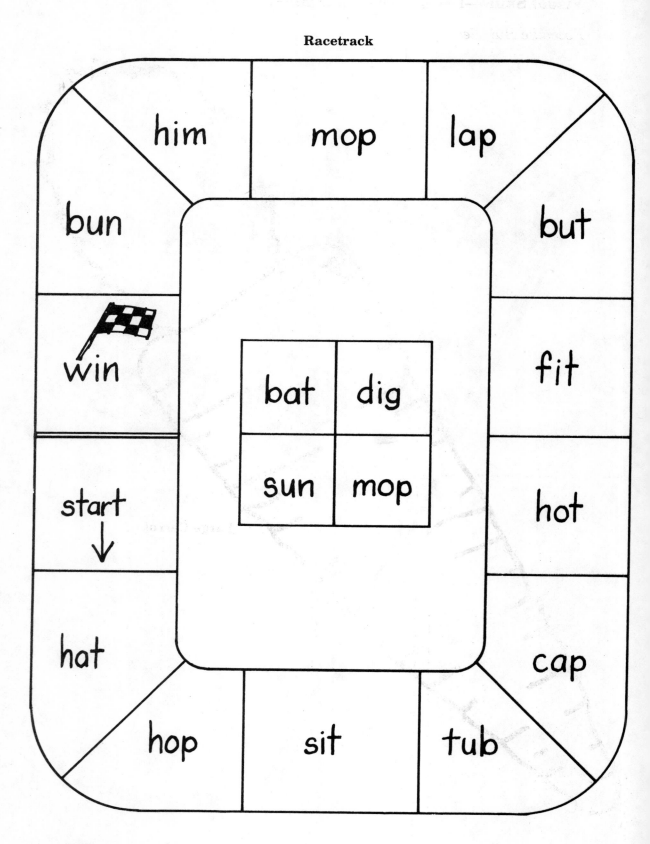

Visual Skills—Level 3 (Discrimination)

Feed the Bunnies

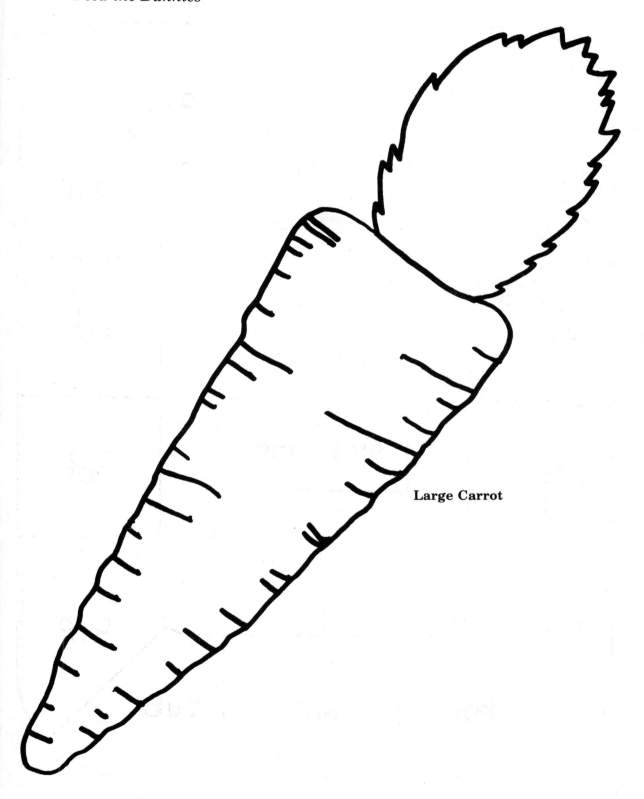

Large Carrot

Bunny, Basket, and Small Carrot

Visual Skills—Level 3 (Discrimination)

Going Fishing

Large Fish

Fish Bowl

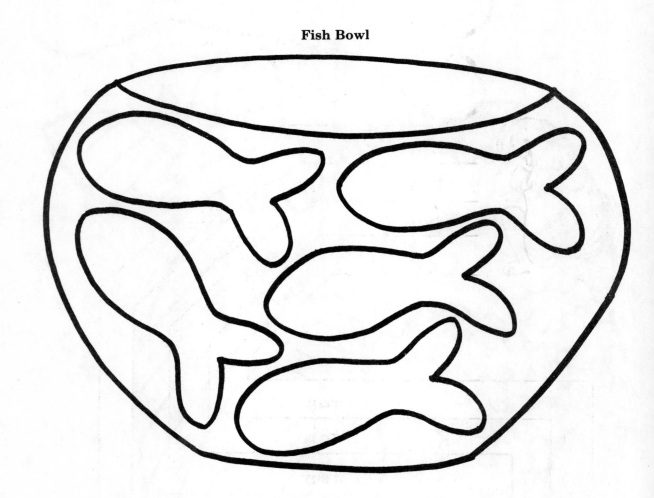

Small Fish

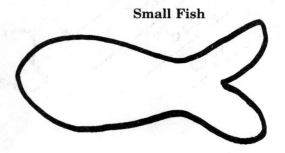

ACTIVITY 32

Visual Skills—Level 3 (Discrimination)

Bumpy's Bone

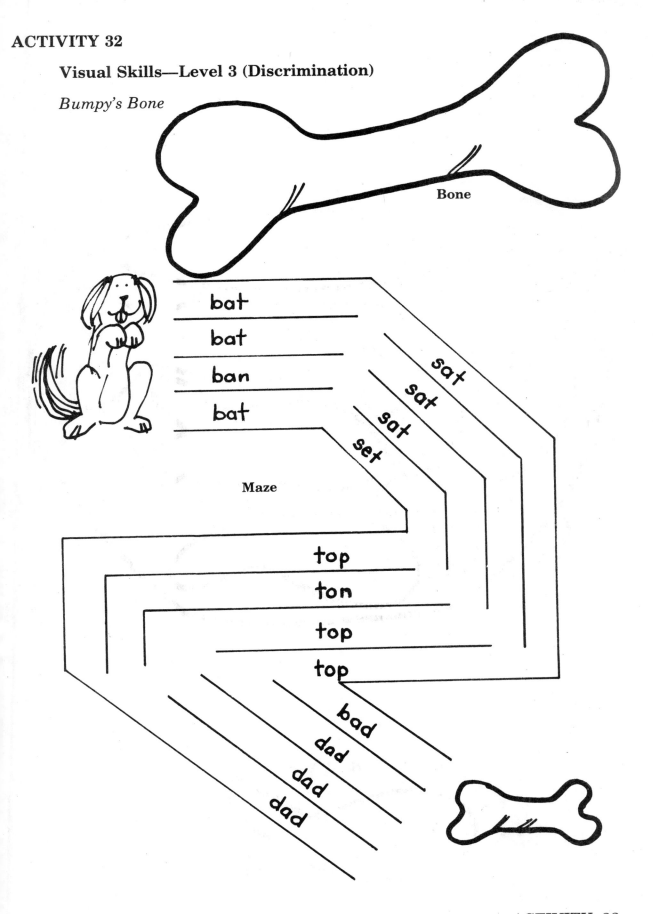

Bone

bat
bat
ban
bat

Maze

sat
sat
sat
set

top
ton
top
top

bad
dad
dad
dad

Picking Apples

Tree

Apple Cards

Word Cards

rea	eta
rae	aer
tae	are
tre	ter
eat	rte